Kant's Analogies of Experience

Arthur Melnick

Kant's Analogies of Experience

The University of Chicago Press
Chicago and London

ARTHUR MELNICK is assistant professor of philosophy at the University of Illinois, Urbana   [1973]

The University of Chicago Press, Chicago 60637
The University of Chicago Press, Ltd., London
© 1973 by The University of Chicago
All rights reserved. Published 1973
Printed in the United States of America
International Standard Book Number: 0–226–51964–3
Library of Congress Catalog Card Number: 73–77138

To Betty and Julius

Contents

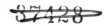

Preface

The aim of this book is to present an account of Kant's argument in the Analogies of Experience. Special emphasis is given to the Second Analogy, the theory of causality that Kant presents in the Analytic. More than usual care is given to the discussion of the details of his causal theory such as, for example, the simultaneity of cause and effect, the relationship between causality, accidental occurrences, and teleology, the distinction between causation and interaction, and the connection between causation and the hypothetical form of judgment. Kant's views on space and time and judgment are discussed to the extent that these views form the background in terms of which his causal theory is to be understood.

This book originated as a Ph.D. thesis at the University of Chicago. I am grateful to the many philosophers there with whom I had the opportunity to discuss Kant; in particular Gale Justin, Earl Ludman, and, at a later date, Nick Georgialis. I also wish to express thanks to Ralf Meerbote for many fruitful exchanges. My most important debt of gratitude is due to Manley Thompson who, both as my thesis adviser at Chicago and afterward, was always my most sympathetic and critical reader. It is no understatement to say that the general outline and many of the details put forth here grew out of many long conferences with Professor Thompson. Thanks are also due to the University of Illinois for a Summer Faculty Fellowship giving me the time to make important revisions, and to the Ford Foundation for a dissertation fellowship under which the work was begun. I am also grateful to Sheila Clair for her efficiency and patience in typing and retyping.

Introduction

In this work I am concerned to defend Kant's claim that the employment of the relational categories and, most important, the concept of causality are necessary if experience is to be possible. Our right to employ the relational categories is, perhaps, the most carefully argued instance of Kant's central claim in the *Critique of Pure Reason* that synthetic a priori modes of knowledge are justifiable; i. e., that certain concepts are a priori and that their employment in experience can be justified.

Certainly much of the section on the Analogies (the section where Kant specifically argues for the validity of the relational categories) would be difficult to understand apart from the rest of the *Critique*. It is also true that certain aspects of this section present difficulties precisely when the Analogies are viewed in relation to other sections of the *Critique*. It seems that certain essential tenets of the section on the Analogies are either in contradiction to, or in a state of uneasy dissociation with, Kant's views in the Aesthetic and the Metaphysical and Transcendental Deductions. Chapter I is an attempt to determine the place of the Analogies in the *Critique*.

Part A of chapter I is concerned with the relation of the Analogies to the Aesthetic as regards Kant's theory of space and time. In the Analytic Kant seems to argue that the parts of space and time are prior to (and synthesized into) the whole, whereas in the Aesthetic he seems to hold that the parts of space and time are possible only through the whole. In section 1 I discuss the distinction between, and the relation of, empirical apprehension and pure intuition. I argue that the parts of space and time, as empirically apprehended, are prior to the whole, but that this apprehension is only possible if, as purely intuited, the whole of space and time is prior to the parts. In section 2, I argue that Kant's view of space and time in the Aesthetic as given intuitions is compatible with his views on *construction* of spaces and times in the Axioms of Intuition, once it is realized that in the Axioms Kant is not saying that space and time are themselves constructed but rather that figures in space and time are constructed. Section 2 also goes on to investigage certain general problems in Kant's theory of space as it relates to mathematics.

In the Analogies, the argument for our right to employ the relational categories hinges on their function as conditions of time determination. This has seemed to some to commit Kant to a relational theory of space and time, which is seen as conflicting with the absolute theory that Kant holds in the Aesthetic. Section 3 of part A is concerned to reconcile this apparent conflict. It is argued that Kant in the Analogies does not hold a relational theory of time, but rather a relational theory of the determination of position in time, and that this latter is compatible with the absolute theory he holds in the Aesthetic. Further, we discuss why Kant holds that temporal relations between objects cannot be reduced to real relations between objects and, perhaps, a more significant question, why time itself cannot be analyzed in terms of temporal relations between objects.

In part B I discuss the relation of the Metaphysical and Transcendental Deductions to the Analogies. Unlike the problem of the relation of the Analytic to the Aesthetic, the problem of the relation between the Deductions and the Analogies is not so much that these sections seem to express conflicting views, as that they seem to express unconnected views. Section 4 deals with the nature of judgment. It is argued that all judgment involves an objective connection and that this is what distinguishes a connection of concepts in a judgment from a connection of concepts that is not a judgment. In sections 5 and 6 I analyze the Metaphysical and Transcendental Deductions. We argue that the former is concerned to show the a priori character or nature of the categories, while the latter is concerned with deducing the objective validity of, or our right to employ, the categories. The central notion in both sections is that of an *epistemic* concept. We argue that the Metaphysical Deduction shows that *a*) the categories are concepts that apply to what is given only insofar as what is given is brought under certain forms of judgment. We then argue that this is, in one sense, sufficient to show the a priori nature of the categories. We argue that in the Transcendental Deduction it is the converse of claim *a* of the

Metaphysical Deduction that is important, namely, *b*) that what is given can be brought under certain forms of judgment only if the categories apply to what is given. In other words, the categories must apply to what is given if what is given is to be an object of judgment. We also argue that the subject distinguishes himself from what is given to him primarily by making what is given to him into an object of judgment (i.e., by judging about what is given to him). Thus, if we are to have a type of consciousness in which we can distinguish what we are conscious of from our consciousness of it, we must be able to judge about what is given to us, and thus the applicability of the categories, as conditions of such judgment, are conditions of such a type of consciousness. In this way the employment of the categories is a condition of ". . . experience as distinguished from mere intuition or sensation of the senses" (*Critique of Pure Reason,* hereafter CPR; B 219, p. 209) and this is a sufficient deduction of them.

In section 7 I discuss the relation of the Metaphysical and Transcendental Deductions to the Analogies. I argue that in the Analogies the relational categories are shown to be conditions of judgment about what is given in experience, by being shown to be conditions of time-determination. Thus, their being conditions of judgment is not, as in the Transcendental Deduction, based on their epistemic character; i.e., their character as concepts that bring what is given under certain judgment forms. I offer a reason why Kant, in the Analogies, gives a new proof of the relational categories, when their validity has supposedly already been shown in the Transcendental Deduction.

The relational categories are characterized in the *Analogies* as concepts whose employment is required for the general possibility of determining time position. The First Analogy argues that the employment of the concept of substance is a condition of determining time magnitude. In section 8 I argue that determining time magnitude is presupposed in all determination of time-position. I argue that this determination cannot be carried out with reference to empty time, but must be based on some feature of appearances. I then argue that only if appearances are brought under the concept of substance (substance being the permanent in appearance) is it possible to determine time magnitude.

In section 9 a different argument for the indispensability of bringing appearances under the concept of substance is offered, based on the idea that changes would be empirically unverifiable unless conceptualized as changes in state of substances.

Causality and interaction are concepts that must be employed if time-order (succession and coexistence, respectively) is to be determinable. In sections 10 and 11 I argue that perception alone is never sufficient for determining the position of appearances in time. In section 12 I offer a reconstruction of the argument of the Second Analogy. It is argued that *1*) Kant shows that since time-position (in this case, succession) cannot be determined either in terms of perception or by reference to empty time, that therefore the determination of time-position must be based on or inferred from features of appearances, but *2*) a rule that enables us to order appearances as successive on the basis of features of appearances is just the core notion of a causal law.

This reconstruction, far from committing Kant to what Strawson has called a "non sequitur of numbing grossness" (Strawson, 1966, p. 137; see Bibliography for full reference) in passing from the necessary order of perceptions to necessity in the order of events perceived, rather depends precisely on the idea that no such transition from perceptions (whether irreversible or not) to objective causal connections is possible.

In section 13 I present an analogous reconstruction of the Third Analogy, this time in relation to coexistence rather than succession. In section 14 I argue that the (very possibly universal) simultaneity of cause and effect is compatible with the function of causal rules as determining succession. In section 15 I discuss the distinction between x causing y *versus* x and y being in mutual interaction. I argue that this distinction can be maintained even if we grant that a cause always interacts with the effect. I claim, however, that the distinction between causality and interaction cannot be correlated, as Kant implies, with determining succession and determining coexistence respectively, for succession can be determined in accordance with laws of interaction and coexistence can be determined in terms of causal laws. Therefore, the conclusion of the Second and Third Analogies must be fused into the claim that the concept of causal connection (in a generic sense that includes interaction as one species; causal connection in this sense being synonymous with real connection according to rules) must be employed if time-determination (both succession and coexistence) is to be possible. In section 16 I discuss the notion of an accidental occurrence. I argue that such occurrences can be analyzed in a way compatible with the thoroughgoing determinability, according to causal laws, of all succession and coexistence. Thus, unless Kant's argument in the Analogies is shown to be invalid (independently of bringing up cases of accidental occurrences), such occurrences must be analyzed in the way suggested. In section 16 I argue that Kant's position in the Second Analogy, that effective causation is the sole and universal principle of time-determination, is compatible with his position in the third *Critique* that teleological judgment is a distinct and indispensible principle of causality. Finally, in section 18 I discuss the necessity and universality of causal connections. I argue that the necessity and universality derive from the use (or function) of causal laws as rules for determining time-order.

There are two opposed views of the connection of Kant's doctrines of transcendental idealism to Kant's justification by transcendental argument of the objective validity of the categories. On the one hand is Strawson's view that "this doctrine [that necessary features of experience have their source in the subject] is incoherent in itself and masks, rather than explains, the real character of his inquiry; so that a central problem in understanding the *Critique* is precisely that of disentangling all that hangs on this doctrine from the analytical argument which is in fact independent of it (Strawson, 1966, p. 16). On the other hand there is Stroud's view that "Surely there is no plausibility at all in the claim to have established ontological conclusions about the way 'objective reality' must be and to have done so simply by reflecting on the conditions of the possibility of experience or language, if the question of whether 'objective reality' is this or that way is thought to be determinately settled one way or the other completely independently of the way we experience, conceive, or talk of it. Transcendental deductions and the Copernican revolution go hand in hand" (Stroud, 1972, p. 25). Chapter IV is an attempt to set out an interpretation of the doctrines of transcendental idealism that make these doctrines an integral part of the complete justification of the categories, i.e., an interpretation more in line with Stroud than Strawson. After some preliminary remarks in section 19, it is argued in section 20 that the subject contributes elements to experience just in the sense that the activity of the judging subject contributes to (forms part of) the concept of these elements. This interpretation of the "contributing relation" arises naturally out of the characterization of the categories in the metaphysical and Transcendental Deductions, and out of the defense of causality in the Second Analogy. In section 21 the notion of a thing in itself is defined as a different kind of concept of a thing than our concept of a thing. The role that such a notion plays as a limiting concept is then discussed. Finally in section 22 it is argued that the justification of the categories depends not merely on their being concepts indispensable for all experience, but also on their being formal concepts. The interconnections of these three notions, viz., the "contributing relation," the notion of a thing in itself, and the notion of a formal element are then discussed in relation to the distinction between transcendental *versus* empirical idealism.

1   *The Place of the Analogies in the Critique*

A. The Aesthetic and the Analytic

Kant's theory of space and time in the Aesthetic has seemed to some to be incompatible with his theory in the Analytic. One apparent discrepancy is that in the Aesthetic it is claimed that the parts of space and time are possible only through the whole, whereas in the Analytic it is claimed that the apprehension of space and time is possible only through a synthesis of given parts. The requirement of synthesis relates both to the empirical apprehension of extents of space and time and the pure construction of figures in space. A second discrepancy is that in the Aesthetic Kant seems to hold an absolute theory of space and time whereas in the Analytic he seems to hold a relational theory. Related to this second point is the fact that Kant sometimes seems to hold that formal (spatial and temporal) relations of objects are prior to real (dynamical) relations of objects, whereas at other times he seems to hold the exact opposite.

In part A of this chapter we attempt to reconcile these apparent conflicts. In section 1 I discuss the "part-whole" controversy as it relates to empirical apprehension, in section 2 as it relates to mathematical construction. In section 3 I discuss the question of whether Kant holds a relational theory of space and time in the Analogies.

1. Pure Intuition and Empirical Apprehension

Kant says, "The quite general representation of the series of all past states in the world as well as of all things which coexist in cosmic space, is itself merely a possible empirical regress which I think to myself though in an indeterminate manner . . . we have the cosmic whole only in concept, never, as a whole in intuition"

(CPR, A 518, B 456, pp. 455–56). Yet he also says, "Space should be properly called not a *compositium* but *totum,* since its parts are possible only in the whole, not the whole through the parts" (CPR, A 438, B 466, p. 405). The former conception of space and time seems to be prevalent in the Analytic (and Dialectic) while the latter is prevalent in the Aesthetic.

Kemp Smith says,

> The arguments by which Kant proves space to be an *a priori* intuition rest on the view that *space is given* as *infinite* and that its *parts arise through limitations* of the *prior existent whole.* But a principle absolutely fundamental to the entire *Critique* is the counter principle that all analysis rests upon and presupposes a previously exercised synthesis. *Synthesis, or totality as such can never be given.* Only in so far as a whole is synthetically constructed can it be apprehended by the mind. *Representation of the parts precedes and renders possible representation of the whole* (Kemp Smith, 1918, p. 45).

In order to see that Kant's theory of space and time in the Aesthetic does not, in this regard, contradict his theory in the Analytic, we must understand the distinction and connection between our (a priori) intuitions of time (and space), and our (empirical) apprehension of appearances in space and time.

In pure intuition, the whole of space and time is prior to its parts. The claim that space, for example, is prior intuitionally to the parts of space is not the (absurd) claim that I can only empirically perceive appearances occupying some part of space by perceiving the whole of space in which all appearances are given. For Kant I could never perceive the whole of space in which appearances have location. Any region of space in which objects are perceived I must imagine as enclosed in larger regions of space that I am not perceiving. My intuition of space is of an unlimited magnitude. Now it is precisely unlimited magnitudes that cannot be perceived. We can only perceive appearances in definite regions of space, regions of space that are bounded or limited by other regions of space that are outside our perceptual field. We cannot imagine space as exhausted by any region of space enclosed within perceptual limits. Kant says of time, "The infinitude of time signifies nothing more than that every determinate magnitude of time is possible only through limitations of the single time that underlies it" (CPR, A 32 – B 48, p. 75).

Our intuitions of space and time are intuitions of the space and time in which appearances are given in perception. There is not one space and time that we intuit and another space and time in which appearances are empirically apprehended. We do not successively perceive appearances occupying different spaces and times but rather different parts of one space and time; i.e., our successive perceptions are against the (intuitive) background of a single space and time. It is only against this background that we can think, e.g., of there being different spaces at all. Part of the claim that the whole of space and time is prior to the parts is that we imagine two regions of space as being numerically distinct only in virtue of their positions relative to one another (their lying outside one another) in one space. Unless we imagine two spaces as being parts of one space, we cannot distinguish the spaces as numerically different, for their only difference is their relative position in the one space of which they are two parts. Kant says, "The concept of a cubic foot of space, wherever and however often I think it, is in itself thought as one and the same. But two cubic feet are nevertheless distinguished in space by mere difference in their locations (*numero diversa*) ..." (CPR, A 282, B 338, p. 289). Again he says, "Space is the form of the external intuition of this sensibility and the internal determination of every space is only possible by determination of its external relation to the whole of space of which it is a part. . . ." (*Prolegomena to Any Future Metaphysics,* hereafter P; p. 40).

The whole of space is prior to the idea that we can distinguish (or even imagine as different) spaces and times (as being parts of the whole). If we give up the idea that all spaces and times are parts of a single space and time, we are not left with the idea that there are numerically distinct but unconnected spaces and times, for distinguishing spaces and times as numerically distinct is possible only in virtue of their being connected as parts of a single whole. Suppose x and y are two cubic-foot regions. Their being two cubic-foot spaces requires that they be two regions of a single space; x and y are not distinguished insofar as we merely think the concept of a cubic foot of space. If C is any concept and w and w′ are two instances of C, then w and w′ cannot be distinguished in terms of C.

If x and y are two cubic-foot regions of space then, qua falling under the general concept of a cubic-foot region of space, x and y are indistinguishable. If we did not consider the instances of this concept as being different parts of one space, we could not distinguish *different* instances of the concept.

The fact that one cubic-foot region of space is numerically distinct from another is ultimately a matter of its being in a different region of one space. The only difference between the spaces is intuitional; we intuit one cubic-foot region of space as being outside another one (as comprising a different region of space). Spaces can be numerically distinct only by lying outside each other in a single space; i.e., only by being regions of one space. This remains true even if one holds a relational theory of space. In a relational theory space is a system of relations between objects. Parts or regions of space would be parts of this system; i.e., subsystems of relations between objects. Let x and y be two such subsystems; i.e., two sets of objects with associated relations. These subsystems may be qualitatively identical and yet numerically distinct. For example, suppose we have xRyR′z and x′Ry′R′z′. If R and R′ are genuine relations, then it must be possible for different collections of qualitatively identical objects to be in, or to have, these relations. If we claim that it is impossible for two qualitatively identical subsystems to be distinct, then the relational theory will fail to capture a crucial feature of space, namely that two spaces, indistinguishable internally, may yet be distinguished in terms of their relations (their position) in the one space of which they are parts. A homogeneous three cubic-foot region of space is made up of three numerically distinct cubic-foot regions of space whether or not these one cubic-foot regions possess any qualitative (internal or monadic) differences.

Thus, if a relational theory is to be a relational theory *of space,* the distinction between numerical and qualitative identity, characteristic of our intuitions of space, must be preserved. But how are we to think of qualitatively identical subsystems as distinct except by thinking of these subsystems as themselves parts of a single system of relations (taking seriously the idea that they are primarily *sub*systems)? Thus, the notion of systems being numerically distinct though qualitatively identical ultimately presupposes a single system of which all systems are parts or subsystems. We do not first have systems well defined as numerically distinct which we then think of as combining to form one comprehensive system.

Now it is a cardinal tenet of Kant's philosophy of space and time that our empirical perceptions of appearances in space and time conform to our pure intuitions of space and time. Empirical perceptions do not conform to pure intuitions by "duplicating" them in the field of experience. For example, we cannot intuit or imagine space as definitely bounded or as having limits. Our empirical perceptions do not conform to this intuition of space by duplicating it. We do not perceive spatial regions (extents of objects in space) that are limitless or without bounds. Rather, we perceive space under the preconception (or, better, under the *"pre-intuition"*) that the bounded spatial extents we do perceive are parts of a limitless or unbounded space.

The most important of these pre-intuitions that we carry with us (or, as Kant would say, that lie ready in our form of intuition) is that the various spatial regions that we successively perceive are all but parts of one single space (similarly for time). We shall see that this intuition has important consequences in the way in which we judge about objects given to us in experience.

I have argued that the numerical difference of spatial regions ultimately depends on our intuition of spatial regions as being but different parts of one space. The concept "numerical difference" is a relational concept; i.e., we say that x is numerically different from y; we do not say simply that x is numerically different. It will be more convenient to introduce the term "numerically differentiable" as a monadic predicate (syntactically), so that x is numerically differentiable means that it is possible for there to be some y such that y is qualitatively identical to x and yet y is numerically distinct from x. For example, we think of a spatio-temporal object x as being numerically differentiable, but we do not think of the *concept* of x as being numerically differentiable. Two concepts are different concepts only if there is some difference in their definitions or explications. Two absolutely similar concepts are the same concept.

Spatial regions are numerically differentiable. First, if I perceive a certain extent of appearances occupying a certain region, parts of this region are numerically differentiable; this in the sense that I perceive the parts as outside one another. Second, the entire region of my perceptual field is numerically differentiable even though, ex hypothesi, I am not perceiving this region as outside any other region. In the first case my pure intuitions are duplicated in empirical perception in a direct manner. Thus, just as two regions are different because I imagine (or intuit) them as outside one another, so two parts of a region I perceive are different because I empirically perceive them outside one another. In the second case the entire region of my perceptual field is not perceived to be numerically different from any other region by perceiving it as outside any other region. Yet the entire region is just as surely numerically differentiable, and in just the same signification of the term, as its parts. The entire region of my perceptual field is just as much a *part* of space as any part of the region. Being merely part of space is what establishes it as numerically differentiable (i.e., that there may be other numerically distinct parts of space that are "qualitatively" or "monadically" identical to it). But I do not perceive that this entire region is a part of space, for that would involve perceiving regions beyond the entire region of my perceptual field. This entire region is, in a sense, "given" to me as a part of space, and yet I do not perceive it to be a part of space (i.e., it is not empirically given as a part of space). It is my pure intuition that every space is a spatial part, in virtue of which I "interpret" what I perceive as a part of space, and thus as a numerically differentiable region. Our intuitions here surpass (and guide) our empirical perceptions.

This intuition, that spaces may be numerically distinct by being outside one another in one space, has important implications for our conception of objects given in space and for the way in which we judge about such objects. Objects "borrow," so to speak, their numerical identity from the region of space and time they occupy. The distinction between numerical and qualitative identity applies primarily to regions of space and time. Spaces that are exactly alike may yet be numerically distinct because they lie outside each other in one space. That they do lie outside each other is something that is ultimately intuited, not discursively understood. There is no answer to the question, in virtue of what features do two spaces lie outside one another? Two qualitatively identical *objects* in space are numerically different because they are in numerically different regions of space.

> A location *b* can contain a thing which is completely similar and equal to another in a location *a,* just as easily as if the things were inwardly ever so different. Difference of locations without any further conditions, makes

the plurality and distinction of objects, as appearances, not only possible but also necessary (CPR, A 272, B 328, pp. 283–84).

Our conception of an object given to us through experience involves the idea of its being numerically differentiable; i.e., for any object given through experience we think it possible for there to be another object qualitatively identical and yet numerically distinct from it. The basis of this conception is that the spatio-temporal locations of objects given in experience (the places and times at which objects are) are numerically differentiable. The basis in turn of the numerical differentiability of the place and time at which an object is, is that it is part of a single space and time. In other words, our ultimate distinction between numerical and qualitative identity rests upon our intuition that all spaces and times are but parts of one space and time. It is thus that two spaces may be internally indistinguishable and yet numerically distinct (in virtue of being outside each other in space) and that two objects (occupants) may be qualitatively identical and yet numerically distinct (in virtue of occupying numerically distinct places).

> . . . Plurality and numerical difference are already given us by space itself, the condition of outer appearances. For one part of space, although completely similar and equal to another part, is still outside the other, and for this very reason is a different part, which when added to it constitutes with it a greater space. The same must be true of all things which exist simultaneously in different spatial positions, however similar and equal they otherwise may be (CPR, A 264, B 320, pp. 278–79).

It is crucial to realize that Kant is not claiming that the way we determine or ascertain that two objects are numerically different is by determining the places of the objects in absolute empty space, distinguishing two places as thus numerically different, and then "transferring" this numerical difference to the objects that occupy these places. As we shall see, determining the actual position of objects in space (time) is not possible by locating the places of these objects in empty space. What Kant is claiming is that the intuition of a single space (and time) whose different parts are numerically distinct is the basis of our conception of occupants of space (and time) as numerically differentiable individuals and not vice versa. That two spaces, as parts of one space, may be numerically distinct is something intuitively obvious; something that does not require the categories; something that does not even require that we think or imagine space as occupied by anything at all. Further, that two objects may be numerically distinct, though not distinguishable qualitatively, is again intuitively obvious because they may occupy different regions of space. Thus, our basic intuition of space (that spaces are numerically differentiable as being different parts of a single space) is prior to our basic conception of objects in space (that objects in space are numerically differentiable).

2. Mathematics and Space

Kant says in an interesting passage in the Amphibolies,

> Accordingly, Leibniz conceived space as a certain order in the community of substances, and time as the dynamical sequence of their states. That which space and time seem to possess *as proper to themselves, in independence of things,* he ascribed to the confusion in their concepts, which has led us to regard what [Leibniz thought] is a mere form of dynamical relations, as being a special intuition, self-subsistent and antecedent to the things themselves [italics mine] (CPR A 276, B 332, pp. 285–86).

The space and time in which appearances are ordered seem to possess properties that go beyond an abstract representation of the ordering of appearances. Leibniz conceived the spatio-temporal order of appearances as being an abstract (an intelligible) order. He thought the connection of appearances according to their dynamical relations captured the structure of the temporal and spatial order between appearances, and thus that the temporal and spatial ordering of appearances could be replaced by an ordering of dynamical connection. For Kant, certain properties of space and time are not grounded upon the structure of the ordering of the occupants of space and time. These would be properties such as infinite divisibility, indefinite extendability, etc. If an ordering of appearances is to be more than merely an abstract order (which is not uniquely—or categorically—spatial and temporal) then it must be an order of appearances in a space and time that possesses properties going beyond the order properties of the appearances.

If we hold a relational theory of space and time; i.e., if we hold that space and time are nothing but orderings of appearances (objects or occupants), then we are forced either 1) to deny (with Leibniz) that the properties that space and time seem to possess in independence of the ordering of things are anything but illusory, or 2) to claim that all properties that space and time seem to possess in independence of the ordering of things they really possess only in virtue of this ordering. For example, the continuous divisibility of space will either have to be relegated to a mere illusion or confusion, or it will have to be reflected somehow as an order property of things in space and time. If we relegate these seemingly independent properties to mere illusion, then the mathematizability of space is likewise relegated to mere illusion, for those properties that space seems to possess by itself are precisely the properties that make space subject to an elegant mathematization (e.g., infinite divisibility, homogeneity, etc.). On the other hand, if we hold that these properties are included in the order relations of the occupants, then the relational theory of space seems forced to the position that the things related are *points,* not substances or objects. For example, if we attempted to think of the continuity of space in terms of the relations of the occupants, we would need some relation R, holding between the occupants, that captures our intuitions about betweenness; e.g., if x and y are two occupants of space that occupy different regions, then no matter how close x and y are it must be possible for there to be an occupant z between x and y. It seems that the only "things" x and y can sensibly be taken to range over are (mathematical) points. For, if x and y and z have extension (say, of one-one-millionth-cubic-centimeter) then it is not true that no matter how close x and y are it must be possible for there to be an occupant z between x and y, unless the occupants are infinitely divisible into smaller occupants. But how is infinite divisibility to be represented as a relational property? A relation holding between what? Not, certainly, an actually infinite number of parts that together make up or compose the body.

If the occupants are taken to be points, then the relational theory would merely be claiming that all spatial relations are reducible to relations between points. In a sense, this claim is trivial (if a *rela-*

tional theory is to be different from an absolute theory) and Kant could agree with it, except that for Kant the points would be limits or positions, not occupants of space.

For Kant, there are properties of space that go beyond the order relations that hold between what can sensibly be thought of as occupants of space. In this sense, Kant holds an absolute theory of space rather than a relational theory of the nature of space. This in itself does not distinguish Kant from the Newtonians. He says of the latter, "The former thinkers obtain at least this advantage, that they keep the field of appearances open for mathematical propositions" (CPR, A 40, B 57 p. 81). Prima facie, this is a puzzling remark. After all, on the Newtonian conception, how can we know a priori that geometry will apply to the space in which we perceive objects? If space is an objective, self-subsistent entity, how are we to know its properties a priori? We have certain intuitions about what properties space must have, but why must space, as an objective entity, conform to such intuitions?*

There is a sense, however, in which an absolute view of space (whether subjectivist or objectivist) makes the mathematization of space comprehensible in a way that a relational theory does not. According to the absolute view, it is possible for space to possess properties that it does not possess merely in virtue of the relations of its occupants. The properties that make space geometrizable are such that, if space possesses these properties at all, it cannot do so in virtue of the relations of its occupants. Thus, geometry could only possibly apply to space if space has properties that go beyond the order properties of its occupants. Thus, if space is nothing but the order of its occupants (a relational view), then geometry could not apply to space. This point is independent of the question of how we can *know* space to be geometrizable. Only in an absolute theory of space (a theory that allows it as possible that space possesses properties beyond the order properties of its occupants) is it possible for geometry to apply to space, though the possibility of our knowing a priori that geometry applies to space is, for Kant, dependent on a subjective absolute theory.

Let us just note a further point regarding the controversy between absolute *versus* relational theories of space. If one holds a rela-

---

* CPR, pp. 174–75, B 167–68. It seems that the Newtonian view would be the middle course.

tional theory of space in the sense that "mathematical" properties of space are interpreted or analyzed in terms of "physical" properties (dynamical behavior) of bodies, then one is compelled to hold that if the behavior of bodies is "discontinuous" (as asserted in quantum theories) then space is discontinuous; i.e., it would be self-contradictory (if one holds a relational view of space in this sense) to assert that the behavior (motion) of bodies in space is discontinuous, but that space itself is continuous. It does not seem that this is self-contradictory, for mathematical representations of quantum theories continue to make use of the notion of the space-time continuum. The mathematics of space and time does not here seem completely dependent upon (or determined by) physical considerations. One way to take Kant's argument for an absolute theory of space is to say that as long as there is an element in our application of mathematics to the world that is not determined by physical considerations, then a theory that reduces spatial relations to real (dynamical) relations of occupants of space cannot be maintained. Those who would uphold a relational theory must bear in mind that this implies that our mathematical representation of the behavior of objects in space must be identical to our mathematical representation of space itself.

Kant makes remarks in the Axioms of Intuition that seem to conflict with remarks he makes in the Aesthetic. For example, he says, "as intuitions in space and time they (appearances) must be represented through the same synthesis whereby space and time in general are determined" (CPR, A 162, B 203, p. 198). Or again he says, "The synthesis of spaces and times, being a synthesis of the essential forms of all intuition, is what makes possible the apprehension of appearances. . . . Whatever pure mathematics establishes in regard to the synthesis of the form of apprehension is also necessarily valid of the objects apprehended" (CPR, A 166, B 206, p. 200). In the Axioms Kant seems to be saying that space and time (the forms of apprehension or intuition) must be synthesized from their parts, while in the Aesthetic he says that the parts of space and time are only possible through the whole.

I argued in section 1 that the fact that we cannot *intuit or imagine* spaces except as parts of a single space does not conflict with the fact that we can only empirically apprehend greater extents of appearances in space by successively apprehending lesser extents (i.e., that our empirical apprehension is from part to greater part). In the

Axioms, however, Kant seems to be saying that space and time as purely intuited (not merely as empirically apprehended) are only possible through a synthesis (in this case a construction) from their parts. Vaihinger points out this (apparent) conflict, saying,

> However, even if we disregard this, we are still led to the following contradiction: Kant is arguing here [in the Aesthetic] against the position that space is to be regarded as constructed, while in the Analytic he expressly holds that *the formal intuition, the intuitive representation of space,* first owes its existence to a synthesis of the understanding [italics mine] (Vaihinger, 1881–92, 2:224).

Also Wolff: "What is more the proof of the principle [of the Axioms of Intuition] is a flat contradiction of one of the proofs [proof 3, A 25, B 39] employed in the Aesthetic" (Wolff, 1963, p. 228). And Kemp Smith, "The argument [of the Axioms of Intuition] in its first edition statement, starts from the formulation of a view of space and time directly opposed to that of the Aesthetic" (Kemp Smith, 1918, p. 347).

The conflict rests on the fact that Kant seems to be saying in the Axioms that the intuition of space and time (space and time as purely intuited) requires construction. And yet the Axioms are concerned with the construction of figures in space (the construction of determinate spaces) and not with the construction of the space itself within which figures are constructed. Kant says, "I cannot represent to myself a line, however small, without drawing it in thought, that is generating from a point all its parts one after another" (CPR, A 163, B 203, p. 198). I can only draw a line in (against the background of) space. If space were not already given to me (imagined by me), I could not generate the line *from a point.* "Points and instants are only limits, that is, more positions which limit space and time. *But positions always presuppose the intuitions which they limit or are intended to limit*" (CPR, A 169, B 211, p. 204). I could not construct space itself, for any spatial construction can only take place in space. Further, any construction is of something determinate. We represent the indefinite extent of a line, not by the construction of an indefinite line, but by a construction that we imagine ourselves to be able to continue indefinitely. The *original* representation of space is required as a background for any construction in space and thus cannot itself be constructed. Any spatial construction is in the context of an original representation of unlimited space that cannot itself be constructed. Thus, in the Axioms, Kant is not saying that space (as purely intuited) must be constructed from parts. Rather, he is saying that figures (purely intuited) in space must be constructed.

Kant says,

> Empirical intuition is possible only by means of the pure intuition of space and time. What geometry asserts of pure intuition is therefore undeniably valid of empirical intuition. The idle objections that objects of the senses may not conform to such rules of construction in space as that of the infinite divisibility of lines or angles must be given up (CPR, A 165, B 206, p. 200).

Kant's explanation of the applicability of geometry seems to be the following: The same principles involved in the pure construction of determinate figures in space are operative as principles of synthesis in our empirical apprehension of things in space.

And yet it seems false that the same principles are involved in empirical intuition as in pure construction, if this means that we perceive the shape of objects, say, just as we construct shapes or figures in space. We do not perceive the shape of a rectangular cardboard box by first perceiving a point on this box and "generating" the shape part by part from this point.

Our geometrical judgments are based on rules of imaginative construction. The *rule* of construction of the figure (not the visual "look" of the figure) is the foundation of its geometrical properties. It is the rule of construction of triangles and parallel lines that determines the equivalence of the angles of a triangle to two right angles. Through perception we become aware of how the shape of an object looks (or feels), but not the rule of construction of the shape. This rule (and what is necessarily bound up with this rule) is something that is brought to perception. Geometrical concepts are not based on looks (even imagined looks) at all. The look of a square object is qualitatively different from the look of a round object, in the same way that the look of a red object is qualitatively different from the look of a green object. Shapes as perceived are qualities in the same sense as colors. The perceptual shape of an object is not a geometrical property of the object any more than its color is. We do not perceive geometrical properties of the object, nor do we construct perceptual qualities of the object.

If Kant's point in saying that perception involves the same unity of synthesis as is involved in pure construction is that the "look" of an object (the look of its shape) is correlated with the rule of construction of the shape, then it seems that Hume's objection that "the imagination reaches a (visible) minimum, and may raise up to itself an idea of which it cannot conceive any subdivision . . ." (Hume, 1888, p. 27) would be plausible. The look of an edge of a box that is infinitely divisible (or which is subject to a construction whose rule involves infinite divisibility) is not different from the look of an edge of a box that is divisible three million times but no more. Hume is talking about what Kant would call the "empirical" imagination. Kant, however, argues that "the mathematics of space [geometry] is based upon this successive synthesis of the *productive* imagination in the *generation* of figures [italics mine]" (CPR, A 163, B 204, p. 199), not upon the successive synthesis of the *empirical* imagination in the (empirical) *apprehension* of figures.

The difference between Kant's pure productive imagination and Hume's empirical imagination can be brought out by considering the extensive magnitude of an object occupying a region of space so small that the imagination (in Hume's sense) cannot "conceive [visualize] any subdivision." For Kant, the rule of construction involved in the case of a small object is the same as the rule of construction in the case of more easily visualizable objects, the rule being the repeated synthesis of some unit. That the unit may be too small to visualize (because it is smaller than the object that is the visualizable minimum) is, for Kant, irrelevant. We "represent" this unvisualizable unit in our imagination by one that is visualizable. The rule of construction (which refers to the *iteration* of units, not to the size of the units iterated) is independent of whether or not the unit is visualizable (empirically perceivable or imaginable). Thus, that the volume of b is 12 one cubic-meter units, while the volume of a is 12 one-millionth cubic-meter units, does not alter the principle of construction, viz., the addition of numerically distinct units to form a larger whole. For Hume, the units themselves must be actually visualizable.

What do we claim when we say that geometry has application to objects in space? The central point is not, I think, that objects in space have certain looks, but rather that the *measurement* of objects conforms to certain geometrical rules. The question is, what is the relation between measurability and construction? Kant, in the Axioms of Intuition, is talking of the "pure measurability" of objects of empirical intuition. The pure measurability of an object is its measurability only *qua* an object in space, abstracting not only, say, from the color and texture of the object, but also from its real relations (causality and interaction) to other objects. Pure measurability is unaffected by any "irregular" behavior of objects vis-à-vis measuring instruments, for the notion of a measuring instrument does not even come into play. Kant is not concerned with empirical limitations on measuring objects, but ultimately with what it is for an object to be measurable, no matter what allowances must be made for the physical behavior of the object. *What it is for an object to be measurable is that it be an extensive magnitude. Being an extensive magnitude is simply being subject to certain rules of construction* (specifically, the rule of iteration of units). That an object is an extensive magnitude is not a perceptual feature of the object. Rather, it is an imposition of certain rules of imaginative construction. For example, the volume of a cube is purely measurable (is an extensive magnitude) because, and insofar as, it is subject to the rule of construction of the iteration of some unit cube. We imagine the cube as an aggregate of such unit cubes. A crucial feature of pure intuition is involved in this construction, namely that when two unit cubes are adjoined they occupy a region of space greater than either of the cubes individually; in other words, that when we add part to part what results is a greater part. This requires that the unit cubes be numerically distinct and thus, ultimately, that they be imagined as located outside each other in one space. Thus, our original intuition of space, as a unity of which all spaces are but parts, is presupposed in the iteration of units. It is the fact that this construction is applicable to objects in space that makes the objects extensive magnitudes. What makes this construction applicable is that objects are in that very space to which our pure intuitions (and pure constructions based on these intuitions) are directed. It is because objects are in space that they are extensive magnitudes. It is because our intuitions and rules of construction apply to the space in which objects are given that objects given to us, *qua* occupying this space, are subject to certain rules of construction and thus are extensive magnitudes.

The crucial problem for Kant's theory of geometry is to give sense to this notion of "pure measurability" where an object is purely measurable if it is subject to a construction by an iteration of units. The following is an elaboration of the problem, not a part of the solution. The distinction is between extensive magnitude per se (pure measurability) on the one hand, and physical measurement plus computability on the other. When we measure an object with a physical instrument, questions regarding the behavior of the object and instrument are relevant. When we compute the magnitude of an object from direct measurements performed on other objects, we do so both in terms of some geometry and some physical theory. Usually, when we think of applying geometry to the world, we are thinking in terms of applying it as a system of rules for *computing* magnitudes, not for directly measuring them. Thus, I measure two angles of a triangular configuration and compute the magnitude of the third angle. The result of my computation will depend on whether the configuration is taken to be Euclidean or Riemannian. Which geometry we use may depend on the pervasive behavior of objects. That objects act according to Euclidean laws (i.e., that their behavior is such as to make Euclidean geometry the most convenient) is, perhaps not a priori decidable. Yet there does seem to be room for Kant's conception of pure measurability as somehow a more fundamental aspect of the applicability of geometry to the world. If an object is computed to have length l in terms of Euclidean geometry and length l' in terms of Riemannian geometry, then if we are to say that we have two computations of the *same* property (i.e., two *conflicting* computations), extensive magnitude must have some signification in abstraction from the behavior of objects and the rules of computation based on a particular geometry.

3. *Relational* versus *Absolute Time*

T. K. Swing, discussing the Second Analogy, says,

> But Kant cannot accept the causal theory of time without abandoning his own doctrine of pure intuitions because the causal theory of time is a special version of the relative theory of time. One of the central features in his doctrine of time as a priori intuition is the claim that temporal relations are prior to or independent of the contents of time. Within this theory of time, it is impos-

sible to maintain that the objective temporal order is equivalent to the causal order or that the latter is indispensable for coming to recognize the former (Swing, 1969, pp. 151–52).

In one sense, the causal theory of time may be characterized as asserting that statements of temporal relations between objects can be analyzed or reduced to statements of real (dynamical) relations between objects. It is in this sense that a causal theory of time would be a special case of a relational theory of time, but it's this type of a causal theory of time that Kant never holds. Swing seems to think that a theory that asserts that temporal relations between objects can only be ascertained in terms of real relations between the objects is identical to a causal theory of time in the sense just defined. Now Kant does hold that what the position of an object in time is can only be determined in terms of dynamical relations between objects. He says, "What determines for each appearance its position in time is the rule of the understanding through which alone the existence of appearances can acquire synthetic unity as regards relations of time" (CPR, A 215, B 263, p. 237). Yet Kant denies that temporal relations between objects can be analyzed in terms of real relations between objects. He makes a distinction between formal or ideal (spatial and temporal) relations on the one hand, and real relations (causality and interaction) on the other and says that we cannot argue from the former to the latter.* We can only argue from the empirical knowledge of the former to the latter. In other words, he holds that we could not determine temporal relations except in terms of real relations of objects, but he does not hold that we can analyze temporal relations in terms of real relations.

Swing, as far as I can see, gives no argument for the claim that the theory 1) that we can only determine temporal relations in terms of real relations implies or is identical to the theory 2) that temporal relations are identical to (or can be analyzed in terms of) real relations of objects. In other words, though 2 is a bona fide relational theory of time and, therefore, incompatible with Kant's remarks in the Aesthetic, it seems clear that a) Kant himself wants to hold 1 but not 2, and that b) 1 is not, prima facie, a relational theory of

---

* Ibid. See, e.g., n. a, A 218, B 265, p. 238.

time at all. (Kant does not hold a relational [causal] theory of time. See W. A. Suchting, "Kant's Second Analogy of Experience," reprinted in *Kant Studies Today*, L. W. Beck, ed.; pp. 338–39.) It is, we may say, a relational theory of determining the position of objects in time. As an analogy, if someone holds that we can only determine whether someone is in pain in terms of verbal and physical behavior, it does not follow that he holds that pain is identical to (or can be analyzed in terms of) such behavior. In a sense the burden of proof is not on Swing but on Kant; i.e., Swing might be saying that someone who holds 1 ought to hold 2 because of some such general line of thought as the following: If we can only determine x in terms of y, then what sense does it make to say that x is anything over and above y? Unless we can give an account of what sense it does make to say x is something more than y, then merely reiterating that the distinction between i) x can only be determined in terms of y, and ii) x can be analyzed in terms of y is unhelpful (though this distinction is valid). In other words, we must see in the particular case of reductionism at hand; i.e., reducing temporal relations to real relations, what reasons Kant has for saying that temporal relations between objects, though only determinable in terms of real relations, are still not identical to or analyzable in terms of these real relations.

The most important of Kant's reasons is that real relations of objects such as causality and mutual interaction can themselves only be understood in terms of temporal relations. He says, "If I omit from the concept of cause the time in which something follows upon something else in conformity with a rule, I should find in the pure category nothing further than that there is something from which we can conclude to the existence of something else. In that case not only would we be unable to distinguish cause and effect from one another, but since the power to draw such inferences requires conditions of which I know nothing, *the concept would yield no indication how it applies to any object* [italics mine]" (CPR, A 243, B 301, p. 262). The notion of causality, if it is to apply to objects, must be applied to objects that are "already" in time, and so the concept itself must be schematized. The unschematized category of causality is merely a concept of the dependence of one thing upon another. The only way we can understand one thing to depend upon another is in terms of change of state and action. A change of state in one thing depends upon the action of another upon it. But both change of state and action are themselves notions that are incomprehensible except as involving temporality.

It is *schematized* categories that are applied to objects. We cannot analyze temporal relations into real relations, for real relations themselves involve temporal notions. Unless we already "understood" (intuitively) the notion of temporal succession, we could not understand the notion of causality as affirming succession according to a rule, or dependence of one event upon another in time.

The idea of applying concepts or relational terms to objects always already requires temporality. If we wished to analyze temporal relations between objects in terms of real relations, then these real relations themselves would have to be understood apart from temporal relations between objects. For Kant we can only understand these relations as holding of objects having temporal relations to other objects. The point is not merely that 1) these relations can only be understood as *applying* to temporal items, but that 2) in order to so apply them, the relations themselves must be schematized; i.e., analyzed (partially) in temporal terms.

> Space and time contain a manifold of pure *a priori* intuition, but at the same time are conditions of the receptivity of our mind—conditions under which alone it can receive representations of objects, *and which therefore must always affect the concepts of these objects* [italics mine] (CPR, A 77, B 102, p. 111).

To say that temporal relations are reducible (without circularity) to real relations would require reducing temporal relations between objects to unschematized real relations between objects (i.e., the reduction would have to be carried out in terms of the *unschematized* categories of causality, substance, and interaction). On the other hand, if we say that temporal relations between objects can only be *determined* in terms of real relations between objects, no circularity is introduced if these real relations are themselves defined (or the criteria of their application is defined) in terms of temporal notions. For example, the statement, "Unless the temporal succession of states of affairs were in accordance with a rule, we could not determine temporal succession" involves no circularity. On the other hand the statement, "The temporal succession of states of affairs *is* (is analyzable in terms of) temporal succession in accordance with a rule" is, as an analysis, circular.

Wolff, in the following passage, hints at an objection similar to, but not quite the same as, Swing's objection. He says,

> The difficulty with this argument is that it denies its own premise. If pure time contained a manifold which could be intuited *a priori,* then it would be possible to establish the time-position of appearances by relation to absolute time. If, on the other hand, time-position can only be established by a process of reciprocal interrelation of the contents of time, then what sense does it make to speak of a pre-existent time order being "carried over" into appearances? (Wolff, 1963, p. 263).

Wolff seems to be making the following point: In the Aesthetic, Wolff is saying, Kant is committed to holding an absolute theory of the determination of the position of objects in time ("If pure time . . . by relation to absolute time") whereas in the Analytic Kant holds a relational theory of the determination of the position of objects in time. Unlike Swing, Wolff does not, in this passage, confuse a theory of time (of what temporal relations are, or how they are to be analyzed) with a theory of the determination of the position of objects in time (of how the position of objects in time is to be ascertained). Yet, in a sense, Wolff seems to be saying that he does not see what a theory of time is supposed to be unless it is a theory of how we determine what the position of objects in time is; i.e., he seems to be implying that Kant's claim that we have an a priori intuition of time can only be understood as the claim that we determine the position of objects by reference to (our intuition of) absolute time.

There is no evidence whatsoever that in the Aesthetic Kant meant to imply that we can determine what the position of an object in time is, by relating the object to absolute time, which we purely intuit. Kant's claim in the Aesthetic seems to be rather that we can only intuitively understand what it is for an object to have position in time (not that we can intuitively determine what actual position the object has). Spatiality and temporality are, for Kant, ineluctably intuitive and are not to be understood discursively in terms of concepts. On the contrary, all application of concepts can only be understood in terms of spatiality and temporality; i.e., as referring to objects in space and time.

The Aesthetic establishes that the fact that what is given to us *has* position in space and time is due to the fact that space and time are forms of our sensibility. Further, *what it is or what is signified by saying* that an object has position in space and time is ultimately traceable to our intuitions regarding space and time. For example, we saw in section 1 of this chapter that our idea of the numerical differentiability of appearances is based on our idea of the numerical differentiability of spaces and times as parts of one space and time. All this is prior to and independent of the question how it is (or in what way) we can determine what the actual position of an object in time is. The Aesthetic tells us that all objects have position in time and that what it is for an object to have position in time can only be intuitively grasped. It does not tell us that we determine which position an object has by relating it intuitively to absolute time.

It seems to me that we can very well understand (grasp) what it is for an object to be in time, without being able to determine what its position in time is. For example, we can understand the following claims without having any idea of how to go about determining when the events *a, b, c* actually occurred:

1) If *a* and *b* have temporal position, then *a* is either before, simultaneous with, or after *c*.

2) If *a* is before *b*, and *b* is before *c*, then *a* is before *c*.

3) If *a* and *b* have temporal position, then the time interval between *a* and *b* is measurable.

4) If *a* has temporal position *t*, then it is possible for there to be an event *a′* exactly like *a* in every respect, except *a* takes place at a different time *t′*.

5) if *a* takes place at *t*, and *a′* takes place at *t′*, then *a* and *a′* cannot be numerically the same event. In this sense, the claim that we have intuitions about time-position, or about objects *qua* their having position in time, is independent of the question of how it is possible to go about determining the actual position of objects in time.

When we determine the actual position of objects in time, this determination conforms to our intuitions of time-order. For example, let us suppose that someone is investigating a murder. From certain evidence he concludes that the victim must have staggered into the kitchen after being hit on the head with the gun. From certain other evidence he concludes that after staggering into the kitchen he must have hit his head on the refrigerator. Suppose now the coroner's evidence indicates that the victim must have hit his head on the refrigerator before being hit on the head with a gun. The investigator will thereby be forced to the position that he has gone wrong somewhere in his conclusions. His reconstruction of the events does not conform to the transitivity of temporal ordering and thus is not a coherent (possible) reconstruction. He knows that he could not be right in his determination of the temporal order of events, for he knows that, whatever else, his determination of temporal order must conform to his temporal intuitions (here, transitivity). Yet the investigator certainly does not determine the temporal order of events intuitively.

Our intuitions about temporal order are "carried over" into the actual order of appearances in the sense that the actual order of appearances as determined in time must conform to our intuitions regarding temporal ordering. It is not a "preexistent time-order" that is carried over; i.e., it is not the case that we intuitively apprehend the actual order of appearances in relation to absolute time.

Wolff, in another passage, raises a more subtle problem. He says,

> Therefore if we seek to set a representation in objective time, we cannot do so by attaching it to a preexisting point of time. The only thing that can be done is to set it in its objective time-relations to other representations. In this way an objective time-order is constructed and that *is* objective time (Wolff, 1963, p. 244).

Here "objective time-order" (which, according to the previous sentence refers to objective time relations between representations; i.e., objective time relations between the contents of time) is identified with objective time itself. Objective time is said to be nothing but objective temporal relations between objects. We have denied that temporal relations between objects can be analyzed in terms of real relations between objects because real relations can only be understood in terms of these temporal relations. Wolff, in this passage, hints at a more subtle form of reductionism, viz., that time can be reduced or analyzed in terms of temporal relations between objects. In a sense this may seem like a trivial reduction, hardly a reduction at all. But there is a sense, I think, in which it is both nontrivial and unKantian, for it seems to imply that what it is for an object to be in time is that it be related temporally to other objects.

In other words, the statement "X is in time' (or, "X has position in time") is to be understood in terms of the statement "X is temporally related to other objects." For Kant, however, I think it would be just the other way around. X is related temporally to other objects because X and these other objects are all in time (or all have position in time). The idea of an object being in time is prior to the idea of it having temporal relations to other objects. The reason I think that Kant would insist on this priority is that any talk of relations between objects presupposes that the objects (the relata) are well-defined apart from the relations asserted to hold between them. To say that X has a certain relation to Y (XRY) seems to imply that X and Y can be specified independently of the relation R. This seems to hold as well for temporal relations. If we say X is before Y, we seem to presuppose that X and Y are specifiable independently of the one being before the other. If this is true, then analyzing time into temporal relations between objects leads to the following difficulty. If "X has a certain position in time" is analyzed as asserting that X is related temporally to other objects, then X and these other objects must be specifiable in independence of their temporal relations. But since (according to the proposed analysis) these temporal relations constitute the relata being in time, the objects would have to be specifiable (or comprehensible) independently of being in time (or having position in time). The impossibility of comprehending something as being an object except if it has temporal position is a persistent motif in the *Critique*. Time cannot be analyzed as being (constituted by) relations between objects (even temporal relations between objects) for this would seem to imply that the objects related are prior to the relations; i.e., that they could be understood as (well-defined) objects independently of these relations. But this would imply that they could be understood as objects prior to imagining or thinking of them in time. Kant says, "Were it [time] a determination or order inhering in things themselves, it could not precede the objects as their condition. . . ." (CPR A 33, B 49, p. 76).

In summary, in this part of the chapter we have attempted to reconcile certain apparent conflicts between Kant's theory of time (and space) in the Analytic and in the Aesthetic. In section 1 we were concerned with the problem of whether the parts of time are prior to and synthesized into a whole or whether the whole of time is prior to the parts. We saw that, *qua* empirically apprehended, the parts are prior; i.e., we apprehend parts of time (stretches of appearances in time) prior to apprehending greater parts (appearances occupying a greater stretch of time). However, this empirical apprehension is under the "pre-intuition" that any part of time empirically apprehended is limited by parts of time that go beyond that apprehension.

In section 2, we were concerned with the problem of whether space is constructed in intuition or rather given in intuition. We saw that construction always referred to the construction of determinate spaces (figures, lines, planes, etc.) and that this construction is always carried out against the background of an original intuition of space that is not itself constructed but rather given.

In section 3 we were concerned with whether Kant holds a relational or an absolute theory of time. We saw that he held a relational theory of the determination of the actual specific position of objects in time, but that this is not to imply that he held a relational theory of time. For Kant, what position an object has in time is determinable only in terms of its real relations to other objects. Nevertheless, what it is for an object to have position in time (what we "understand" by an object having position in time) cannot be analyzed (or reduced) to relations between objects, either real or temporal. It cannot be analyzed in terms of relations between objects, because these real relations are themselves only comprehensible in terms of temporal relations (or as involving temporal relations). It cannot be analyzed in terms of temporal relations because this would imply that the objects related are conceivable independently of these relations and thus independently of having position (or being) in time.

B. The Structure of the Analytic

4. *The Connection of Concepts in a Judgment*

Kant discusses the notion of judgment in section 19 of the second edition Deduction. The title of this section, "The logical form of all judgments consists in the objective unity of the apperception of the concepts which they contain," can serve as Kant's characterization of judgment. He is arguing here that, in some sense, all judgments are "objective," or that a judgment is always "a relation which is objectively valid" (B 142). One way to read this section is to say that Kant concludes that judgments that assert a merely "subjective connection such as, say, a succession of perceptions in me are not judgments at all. But this conclusion seems to me so blatantly wrong that we must see whether Kant does not have something else in mind when he says that a judgment is "a relation which is objectively valid."

Even the way we have formulated the suggested conclusion, viz., judgments that assert a subjective connection are not judgments at all, indicates the absurdity of the claim. How can a judgment that asserts a subjective connection not be a judgment; i.e., how can one kind of judgment not be a judgment at all? A classification of judgments into those that assert connections that are subjective (i.e., connections of something in the subject) *versus* those that assert objective connections cannot be a way of distinguishing what is and what is not a judgment. Yet it is clear that it is this latter distinction with which Kant is concerned. "I have never been able to accept the interpretation which logicians give of judgment *in general* [italics mine]" (CPR, B 140).

According to logicians, judgment is "the representation of a relation between two concepts." Kant's major complaint with this definition is that it "does not determine in what the asserted *relation* consists." In other words, Kant is indicating that not every representation of a relation between two concepts is a judgment, and this, of course, is true. Linguistically, the concepts 'black' and 'man' are related in the phrase "the black man," which does not express a judgment, as well as in the sentence, "The man is black," which does express a judgment. The linguistic indication of a relation of concepts that forms a judgment is the copula "is."

Kant says,

> I find that a judgment is nothing but the manner in which given modes of knowledge are brought to the objective unity of apperception. This is what is intended by the copula "is." It is employed to distinguish the objective unity of given representations from the subjective (CPR, B 142).

What distinguishes judgment from other relations of concepts is that, in some sense, a judgment involves an objective unity of representations. Now what does Kant have in mind in distinguishing the objective unity of representations from the merely subjective unity? From what he has said previously in this section, the term

"representations" in the phrase "the objective unity of given representations" ought to be taken to refer to concepts, for he is asking
what kind of relation between concepts is involved in judgment
(since not any relation between concepts will do—this being his
complaint against the logicians). In other words, a judgment would
involve an objective as opposed to a merely subjective unification of
concepts. What is required is to show a relevant distinction between
an objective and a merely subjective unification of concepts. Pre-
sumably, it is this distinction that Kant gives at the end of the section
where he says we must distinguish an objectively valid relation of
representations "from a relation of the same representations which
would have only subjective validity" (B 142). What he then says
is that "in the latter case [where the representations have only subjective validity] all I could say would be 'If I support a body, I feel
an impression of weight.' " Here he seems to be saying that if the
connection of representations is only subjective (where representations signify something like *perceptions*—the perception of supporting a body and having an impression of weight), then what I assert
has only subjective validity. This, of course, is true in the sense that
if my judgment asserts a connection between perceptions of mine,
then my judgment asserts a subjective connection; i.e., a connection
of perceptions in the subject. It is also true that "to say 'The body is
heavy' is not merely to state that the two representations have always
been conjoined in my perception . . . ," for to assert a connection in
the object is not (prima facie anyway) to assert a repeated connection of perceptions in the subject. But all this is completely irrelevant
to the question of what is and what is not a judgment. It merely
seems to be a distinction between judgments that assert a connection
of perceptions in the subject versus judgments that assert a connection in the object. In fact, Kant seems to be distinguishing here what,
in the *Prolegomena,* he distinguished as judgments of perception
from judgments of experience (P, pp. 55 ff). But he nowhere says
in the *Prolegomena* that judgments of perception are not judgments
at all. What he says is that they are only "subjectively valid judgments" (P, p. 57).

In light of these remarks, what one could do is to take section 19
as being an answer to the question "What is involved in a judgment
that asserts an objective connection?" rather than as an answer to the
question, "What is a judgment in general (whether what it asserts
is an objective or a subjective connection)?" It seems clear that Kant

at least introduces the section as being an answer to the latter question. I see no way in which 1) distinguishing judgments that assert a connection of perceptions from judgments that assert a connection in the object can serve to decide 2) when relations of concepts form a judgment as opposed to when they do not. I wish to argue that Kant does, however, indicate an answer to 2 in this section, and that these last few sentences are a confusion of this answer.

Kant says in a letter to J. S. Beck (3 July 1792),

> The difference between a connection of representations in a concept and one in a judgment, for example, "The black man" and "the man is black" (in other words, "the man *who* is black" and "the man *is* black") lies, I think, in this: in the first one thinks of a concept as *determined;* in the second, one thinks of the *determining activity* of this concept. But you are quite right to say that in the *synthesized* concept, the unity of consciousness should be subjectively given, whereas in the *synthesizing* of concepts the unity of consciousness should be objectively made; that is, in the first, the man is merely *thought* of as black (problematically represented) and in the second he is recognized as black. (Zweig, 1969, p. 192).

Here Kant seems to be distinguishing mere conception from judgment. In judgment, the "determining activity" of the concept is involved. What this seems to mean is that in a judgment a concept is *employed;* i.e., it is applied to some object or it is used to assert something of an object. By 'object' here I mean object of judgment; i.e., that which the judgment asserts something about. Thus, an object of judgment may even be a concept if my judgment is meant to *determine,* that is, say something about, a concept. According to this usage, the object of my judgment may also be my own perceptions; i.e., the judgment may assert something about a connection of perceptions in me.

In a judgment the representations "belong to one another . . . according to principles of the objective determination of all representations, insofar as knowledge can be acquired by means of these representations." In a judgment, concepts are connected to form an assertion about something; i.e., to express (if true) knowledge of the object of the judgment. The merely subjective unity of representations would be the following. In the problematic representation of a black man, I think the concept 'black' *in conjunction with* the concept 'man'; i.e., these concepts are united (subjectively) in my thought (in my mental state). This is not to say that I think (judge) that they are so united, for in merely representing (thinking) a black man, I make no judgment whatsoever, either about a man or about a connection of concepts in me. In representing a black man I am not *determining* that these concepts are so united in my thought (to so determine would involve a judgment). ". . . In the first one thinks of the concepts as determined." That I think one concept in conjunction with another is not to say that I think the one as being conjoined or connected to the other either in "reality" or in my thought. It is in judging about concepts ("The concept 'black' is consistent with the concept 'man' ") that I think (judge) that the concepts are connected (as consistent). It is in judging about my mental state (*judging* that I am thinking one in conjunction with another) that I think (judge) one concept as being conjoined with another.

Now this subjective unity of representations (concepts) is also involved in any judgment. If I judge that the man is black, then I am employing the concept 'man' *in conjunction with* the concept 'black'. In the case of judgment I am employing the concepts in conjunction with one another in order to make an assertion, to determine something about something. In employing the concept 'black' in conjunction with the concept 'man', I am (in the case of judgment) asserting that the man is black. Thus there is always an objective unity of representations involved in judgment, in that judgment always involves the assertion of a connection (a unity) not between the concepts employed in making the judgment (though these concepts are connected in my thought in the sense that I am employing one *together with* the other), but in the object of the judgment. If I judge that the man is black, what is *signified* by the concept black' is asserted to be unified (connected) with what is signified by the concept 'man'; there is an asserted unity of being black with being a particular man. This objective unity (the unity asserted by the judgment to hold of its object) is to be distinguished from the mere subjective unity involved in employing the concept 'black' together with the concept 'man', for this subjective unity, as such, does not distinguish the judgment that the man is black from the mere "problematic representation" of a black man. (A problematic representation in this sense of merely thinking concepts together with one another is not to be confused with a problematic judgment, where something is asserted to hold in the object of judgment, but only problematically.)

In a problematic representation, I am thinking one concept together with another. In a judgment this is also true, but further I think (or employ) one concept together with another in order to assert something about some object, where 'object' signifies here that about which I assert something.

In section 19, there are two ways in which Kant resists this interpretation of having provided a distinction between judgment and mere conception. First, it is not clear that in talking of the subjective unity of representations Kant is restricting himself to conceptual representations. Certainly his example of supporting a body and feeling an impression of weight seems to indicate that he means a conjunction or unity of intuitive representations; i.e., perceptions. Now it is true that a mere connection of perceptions is not a judgment. But it is equally true that a body being heavy is not a judgment either. A connection of perceptions in me and a connection in the object are both facts or states of affairs, not judgments. We might take Kant to be indicating by his example of supporting a body (etc.) that the concepts of body and weight, merely thought together, do not constitute a judgment (this would be more appropriate to our interpretation). At the end of section 18 he says, "The empirical unity of apperception, upon which we are not here dwelling, and which besides is merely derived from the former under given conditions *in concreto,* has only subjective validity. To one man for instance, a certain word suggests one thing, to another, some other thing . . ." (CPR, B 140, p. 158). Here he does seem to mean by subjective unity merely thinking concepts in conjunction (one concept suggesting another).

Even if we take Kant to mean by subjective unity merely thinking concepts together, there is the primary difficulty that Kant, in this example of supporting a body, etc., seems to be contrasting my *judgment* about my mental state (whether this mental state be a connection of concepts or of perceptions) with a judgment about an objective state of affairs (a state of affairs distinct from my mental state); i.e., he seems to be distinguishing subjective from objective judgments. This, again, is what is so puzzling if we grant, as I have indicated that we ought, that Kant, in this section, sets himself the task of determining when a relation of concepts is a judgment at all. What I suggest is that we ought to disregard this example as an unfortunate one that obscures the real point of this section (viz., the distinction between judgment and nonjudgment). As we shall see below, it is precisely the distinction between judgment and nonjudgment (not the distinction between judgments that assert something about the mental state of the subject versus judgments that assert something about "physical" states of affairs) that is relevant to the argument of the Transcendental Deduction. Further, it is the confusion of these two distinctions that leads to an interpretation of the Second Analogy as wrongheaded as Lovejoy's that "Kant fully follows Wolff in resting the case for the *a priori* validity of the causal law upon the supposed fact that without it we should have no criterion for distinguishing the purely subjective from the objective in the changes of things" (Lovejoy, 1906; in Gram, 1967, p. 292). What lies behind this interpretation is the idea that causality and the other categories are the foundation of the possibility of making objective as opposed to subjective judgments, whereas I shall argue that the categories' function of bringing representations to the objective unity of apperception refers rather to their function as the foundation of making any kind of judgments at all (see sections 5–6, below). In particular, the concept of causality functions in a way more fundamental than as a ground of the possibility of objective as opposed to subjective judgment. (See pp. 84 ff., below, on why causality does not function as a criterion for distinguishing the subjective from the objective.)

In summary, in any judgment we distinguish what is true of the subject judging from what is true of the object of his judgment. If I judge that the man is black, we distinguish the fact that I am thinking the concepts 'black' and 'man' in conjunction with one another from whether or not the man about whom I am judging is black. This distinction only arises when I connect concepts to form a judgment. If I merely think the concept 'black' in conjunction with the concept 'man', all that can be said is that these concepts are conjoined in my mental state. The question of whether any man is black does not arise. This point, that in judgments we distinguish what is true of the subject judging (the subjective unity of concepts; i.e., that he thinks certain concepts together with one another) from the question of the truth or falsity of the judgment (the asserted objective unity of the judgment; i.e., what the judgment asserts to be connected), does not imply that we cannot judge about our own mental state. If I judge that wormwood is bitter to me, we can distinguish the fact that I think the concepts 'wormwood' and 'bitter' in conjunction with one another from the fact asserted by the judgment, viz., the being bitter of wormwood to me. In a sense, both of these facts are merely about me, about my mental state. And yet we must distinguish what is true of me *qua* the subject who judges (that I think certain concepts together) from what is true of me *qua* the object of judgment (I am judging about myself that wormwood is bitter to me). We must not conclude from the fact that in cases of judgment we distinguish what is true of the subject who judges from what is true of the object of the judgment, that no judgment has as an object the mental state of the subject.

5. *The Metaphysical Deduction*

In the first part of this chapter, I have hinted at one characterization of the function of the relational categories, viz., that their application is a condition of the general possibility of determining the position of objects in time. Synthetic a priori judgments can only be justified if they are shown to be necessary conditions of experience, so the immediate question that arises is how the function of the relational categories as conditions of time-determination implies that the employment of these categories is necessary for experience to be possible.

It is in the Transcendental Deduction that the characterization of the categories as conditions of judgment in experience (i.e., conditions of judging about what is given in experience) is prevalent. Kant says, "The concepts which thus contain *a priori* the pure thought involved in every experience we find in the categories. If we can prove that by their means alone an object can be thought, this will be a sufficient deduction of them, and will justify their objective validity" (CPR, A 97, p. 130). It is in the Analogies of Experience that the characterization of the relational categories as necessary conditions of time-determination is stressed. Kant says, "These, then, are the three analogies of experience. They are simply principles of the determination of the existence of appearances in time . . ." (CPR, A 215, B 262, p. 236). "What determines for each appearance its position in time is the rule of the understanding (the analogy of experience) through which alone the existence of appearances can acquire synthetic unity as regards relations of time" (CPR, A 215, B 262, p. 237).

It is clear, I think, that the more fundamental description of the categories is that they are conditions of judgment about what is given in experience, for the reason that only as being conditions of experience can the categories be justified or shown to have objective validity. The description of the relational categories as conditions of time-determination is relevant or salient to the justification of these categories only insofar as their being conditions of time-determination is, at least in part, the way they function as conditions of judgment in experience. In the second part of this chapter we discuss the connection between the relational categories as conditions of judgment and these same categories as conditions of time-determination.

Kant says, "In the *metaphysical deduction* the a priori origin of the categories has been proved through their complete agreement with the general logical functions of thought . . ." (CPR, B 159, p. 170). The title of the first chapter of the Analytic is, "The Clue to the Discovery of All Pure Concepts of the Understanding," and Kant says about the table of Categories that

> This division is developed systematically from a common principle, namely, the faculty of judgment (which is the same as the faculty of thought). It has not arisen rhap-sodically, as the result of a haphazard search after pure concepts, the complete enumeration of which, as based on induction only, could never be guaranteed. (CPR, A 81, B 107, p. 114).

Thus, there are two functions suggested for the derivation of the categories from the logical functions of judgment:

> 1) The categories are thereby shown to have an a priori origin.
> 2) The completeness of the list of categories is en-sured. The really important function of the derivation, I suggest is 1, and 2 can only be understood in terms of 1 (see p. 42, below). The question is, then, how does it follow from the fact that a concept is associated with a logical function of judgment that the concept is of a priori origin?

The logical functions of judgment are themselves *syntactical* concepts; concepts of judgment forms rather than concepts of the objects judged about. For example, if I judge "the elephant is purple," it is the *concepts* 'elephant' and 'purple' that are related as subject and predicate in the judgment. The actual (or fictitious) elephant is not a subject; it is what is referred to by the subject term of the judgment. The logical functions of judgment are concepts of the unification of terms into judgments, or judgments into more complex judgments.

Now, according to Kant, the syntactical structure of judgments in some sense introduces a nonsyntactical element into our knowledge (in Kant's terminology, it "introduces a transcendental [as opposed to formal] content" [CPR, A 79, B 105, p. 112]. Kant's actual list of logical functions of judgment includes what might nowadays be called quantificational logic (Of Quantity), modal logic (Of Modality) and propositional logic (Of Quality and Of Relation— where the categorical judgment would be the sentential letter p). We shall see eventually that the hypothetical form of judgment is most plausibly construed as being, for Kant, the *nonmaterial* hypothetical, and thus cannot be assimilated correctly under propositional or truth-functional logic.

It is hard perhaps to see how truth-functional connectives can have nonsyntactical counterparts.* Let us take as an example, however, quantification, which Kant introduces as a logical function of judgment under the heading "Of Quantity." Quantification is studied by logicians who derive rules for which sentences can be derived from other sentences based on the quantificational structure of the sentences involved. Thus, $\forall x (Px \& Qx)$ can be deduced from $\forall x Px \& \forall x Qx$. This inference tells us something about the relation between the scope of a universal quantifier and the truth-functional connective of conjunction. In devising such rules the logician is not concerned with what domain the variables range over in the sentences. As soon as we consider, however, how judgments of such form relate to objects rather than how they relate to other judgments (i.e., in Kant's terminology, as soon as we pass from

* See Strawson 1966, p. 81: "There can be no particular way in which we *must* conceive of objects of experience in order for truth-functional composition of statements about such objects to be possible." Also, for Quine truth-functional connectives are amenable to radical translation, which would suggest that for him they are not ontological concepts (Quine, 1960, pp. 57–61).

general to transcendental logic) a domain that the variables range over must be provided; and further, a principle for deciding what is to count as one object of the domain must be supplied. The question, e.g., of whether the sentence is true (a semantical question) depends not only on the domain but on how objects in the domain are individuated. To borrow Quine's example, the spatio-temporal sum of rabbit parts is the same domain as the spatio-temporal sum of rabbits. If the predicate Q is "composed of two legs and two ears," then $\forall x Q x$ is, barring injury or malformation, true if the individuals are taken to be rabbits and false if the individuals are taken to be rabbit parts (a rabbit leg, for example, is not composed of two legs and two ears). Thus, if a subject is going to judge about objects where his judgments have quantificational structure and where it is going to make sense to say that his judgments could be either true or false, he must have some conception of what is to count as an individual or as one object.*

Now the notion of an individual (of one thing) is not a notion that applies to judgments; rather, it is a notion that applies to what is judged about. Thus, the syntactical concepts under the heading "Of Quantity" are intimately connected to the notion of an individual, which is not a syntactical notion at all. Our question is, in what sense is the notion of an individual "derivable" from the corresponding syntactical concepts? Certainly, it is not the case that what is to count as an individual, or what is to count as one object, is deducible from quantificational structure. As we have seen, quantificational structure in itself does not determine whether individuals are to be rabbits or rabbit parts. Closer to the truth is that the very question of what is to count as an individual makes no sense for a subject who does not judge under quantificational (or some functionally equivalent) form. What I wish to suggest is that.

1) The intended relation between each logical function of judgment L and its corresponding category C is that only a subject who judges under the judgment form L can have (and apply) the concept C.

---

* And thus, ipso facto, of what is to count as 2, 3, 4, , , , objects. In this way quantification is connected with quantifying in the sense of counting or being able to determine how many. The heading "Of Quantity" eventually leads for Kant to the notion of extensive magnitude, which is continuous not discrete. Yet even here the notion of an individual (what is to count as one) remains important, in the sense that what is to count as one *unit* is indispensable for measurement.

2) The relationship in 1 makes plausible why the correspondence between the logical functions of judgment and the categories should imply that the latter are of a priori origin.

1) Let us say that a concept C is epistemic if *a*) it is a concept applying to the objects of judgment and if *b*) only a subject with a certain judgment form can so apply or have the concept. Here *a*) distinguishes epistemic concepts from both syntactical and semantical concepts that are concepts of judgment forms rather than concepts of objects of judgment (what is judged about), and *b*) distinguishes epistemic concepts from what I shall call "empirical" concepts, concepts such as red, hard, square, and so on. Thus, for example, the notion of an individual would be an epistemic notion in the sense that an individual is, essentially, the referent of a singular term, and only a subject who judges by means of singular terms (or by means of some functionally equivalent syntactic structure) can be said to have this concept or notion.*

Epistemic concepts apply to what is given only insofar as what is given is brought under a certain form of judgment. This is precisely Kant's conception of the categories. He says, "But first I shall introduce a word of explanation in regard to the categories. They are concepts of an object [as opposed to syntactical concepts of judgment forms] in general, by means of which the intuition of an object is regarded as determined in respect of one of the logical functions of judgment" (CPR, B 128, p. 128). Let us note that to claim that C is an epistemic concept, in that it applies to what is given only insofar as what is given is brought under the logical function of judgment L, is not to claim that every time the subject judges under the L-form that he is thereby employing the concept C or applying C to what is given. What is claimed is the converse; when the subject employs or applies the concept C, he can do so only by bringing what is given under the corresponding judgment form L (see p. 46, below, and pp. 55–56, below).

2) We have described the relation between the categories and the logical functions of judgment as one that purports to establish the

---

*'Truth' is a semantical (rather than syntactical) concept because it applies to judgments, but only *vis-à-vis* what they are judgments of categorically. The categories are epistemic (rather than empirical) concepts because they apply to what judgments are of but only in relation to the forms of judgment.

categories as epistemic concepts. How is this linked to the idea that the derivation of the categories from the logical functions of judgment shows the categories to be of a priori origin? The key idea, I think, is that epistemic concepts cannot be *derived* from what is sensibly given as such in experience, because they essentially involve a relation of what is given to the understanding (judgment). In the same way they do not apply to the sensibly given as such; they only apply to the sensibly given insofar as it is brought under a logical function of judgment. In other words, epistemic concepts are concepts that go beyond what can be sensibly given as such (they are a priori concepts) because they concern the relation of what is given to our forms of judgment. Epistemic concepts, qua making reference to the forms of judgment, are not concepts derivable from sensible affection as such, since sensible affection as such makes no reference at all to judgment forms. For Kant, an a priori concept is one that neither can be derived from nor applied to the merely sensibly given, since it designates what cannot be merely given through sensation. An epistemic concept designates what cannot be given through sensation since it is a concept applying to what is given, not insofar as we are affected through sensibility, but insofar as what is given is to be brought under a certain judgment form.

The other function of the Metaphysical Deduction; i.e., that it supplies a clue for the derivation of all categories, is comprehensible, I think, once it is seen that we are trying to prepare a list of epistemic concepts. It seems to me plausible to say that a clue (perhaps the only clue) to which concepts are epistemic (i.e., which concepts relate to what is given only insofar as what is given is brought under certain forms of judgment) will be found in a list (if available) of these forms of judgment. A pure concept of the understanding is a concept that applies to what is given only insofar as what is given is to be brought under (a judgment form) L. Granted that this is the nature of the pure concepts that Kant is trying to derive, it seems reasonable to search for these concepts through an investigation of the judgment forms that can be substituted for L in the above expression.

6. The Transcendental Deduction

In discussing the Transcendental Deduction I have in mind the B-edition version. In the transcendental deduction Kant is concerned to argue for the *objective validity* of the categories; i.e., he is concerned with our right to employ such a priori concepts in experience. The argument as I shall present it proceeds in two broad stages:

> 1) The notion of an object is reinterpreted as being primarily the notion of an object *of judgment*.
> 2) What is given can be an object of judgment only through the employment of epistemic concepts.

1) The notion of an object for Kant is, we may say, primarily and essentially an epistemic notion. By this I mean that the question of how we can judge about what is given is identical to the question of how what is given can be an *object* for us. In other words, the notion of an object is essentially that of an object *of judgment* (or an object for judgment). The notions of 'judgment' and 'object' are, for Kant, correlative. As we have seen in section 4, judgment always has its object (judgment is always judgment about some object). The novel Kantian thesis is the converse claim that to be an object is essentially to be an object of judgment.

Kant's argument for this claim is one of the central motifs of the Transcendental Deduction. We can do no more than hint at this argument, for it is the implications of this claim (forming the second central motif of the deduction) that are most germane to this work. That the notion of an object is, in some sense, a relative notion is plausible if we think of the correlative notion as being the subject. In other words, the object is what is contrasted as being something distinct from the 'I' or from the subject for which it is the object. It does not follow from the fact that 'subject' or 'object' are correlative in this way that any object depends for existence on any subject. 'Big' and 'small' are correlative terms, and it is certainly possible for any big thing to exist independently of any particular small thing.

Now, for Kant, the subject distinguishes himself from what is given to him essentially through making what is given to him into an object of judgment. It is essentially the *judging* subject that is distinguished from the object of judgment (whether that object be something given through outer sense, i.e., an object in space, or something given through inner sense, i.e., an empirical state of ourselves). It might seem as if characterizing sensible affection in terms of something being *given to* the subject introduces (within sensible affection itself) a distinction between that which is given and that to which it is given. This neglects the fact that characterizing sensible affection as something being given is already to bring in judgment, for something is given only in the sense of "given to be judged about." It is only through judging that I become conscious of something being *given* to me at all and as an object distinct from me (from the 'I' who judges). The basic distinction between subject and object thus becomes, for Kant, the distinction between judgment (the judging, not merely the affected subject) and its object (the object judged about, not the mere sensible affection). Kant says, "For through the 'I' as simple representation, nothing manifold is given; only in intuition, which is distinct from the 'I', can a manifold be given; and only through *combination* in one consciousness [i.e., only through judgment] can it be thought [as distinct from the 'I' that judges]" (CPR, B 133, p. 153; see also B 135, p. 155).

Let us note that Kant does not say that judgment is essential for every form (species) of consciousness. Making what is given into an object of judgment is essential for a form of consciousness in which the subject of consciousness can distinguish himself from what he is conscious of (i.e., in which what is given to him becomes both an object distinct from and for him). We shall argue presently that the categories must be employed if what is given is to be an object of judgment, and thus that the categories are essential for a form of consciousness in which the subject can distinguish himself from what he is conscious of. First, let me point out that Kant nowhere claims that the categories represent the conditions under which a subject can be sensibly affected. He says in section 13, "The categories of understanding, on the other hand, do not represent the conditions under which objects are given in intuition [though they do represent the conditions under which what is given in intuition is to be an object distinguished from the subject]. Objects may, therefore, appear to us [though not *as objects;* i.e., as distinct from the subject] without their being under the necessity of being related to the functions of the understanding . . ." (CPR, A 89, B 122, pp. 123–24). Kemp Smith objects to this passage. He says that the claim that appearances could be given in intuition apart from the functions of the understanding is "Pre-Critical." For Kemp Smith, the categories are conditions of consciousness, period; they are conditions of all sense-experience (Kemp Smith, 1918, p. 222). Let us distinguish three claims:

i) The categories are conditions of being merely sensibly affected;

ii) The categories are conditions of all consciousness;

iii) The categories are conditions of a form of consciousness in which the subject can distinguish himself from what he is conscious of.

It seems clear that in section 13 Kant denies *i*. If we hold that merely being sensibly affected is a form of consciousness, then the denial of *i* implies, contrary to Kemp Smith, the denial of *ii*. The question of whether mere sensible affection is a form of consciousness, however, seems to me one that Kant does not clearly answer, nor one that he need consider. In any case, this question is clearly neutral with respect to Kant denying *i* and holding *iii*, and *iii*, it seems, would be a sufficient deduction of the categories.

2) Kant's major point is that *judgment can relate to what is given in experience (or, what is given in experience can be an object of judgment) only if what is given conforms to certain epistemic categories that set up or define the relation between judgment and what is given sensibly in the first place.* Our knowledge of objects is not exhausted by sensible features given through experience, for these sensible features as such do not constitute what is given as being an object of judgment. It makes sense to say that something red can be given to a subject apart from how that subject conceptualizes about what is given to him. It makes no sense to say that something can be given to him as an object of judgment apart from how the subject conceptualizes about what is given. For example, what is to count as an individual (as the referent of a singular term) is not determined by sensible features or features given to the subject sensibly. In Kant's terminology, epistemic concepts and only epistemic concepts can bring appearances (what is given) into necessary relation to the understanding (the faculty of judgment).

For Kant, the *relation* between *i*), what is given through sensibility, and *ii*), our judging, under certain forms, of what is thus given, is not itself something that can be merely given through sensibility. He says,

Combination [the unity of intuitions that brings them under judgment forms] does not, however, lie in the

> objects, and cannot be borrowed from them, and so, through perception, first taken up into the understanding. On the contrary, it is an affair of the understanding alone, which itself is nothing but the faculty of combining *a priori,* and of bringing the manifold of given representations under the unity of apperception [of bringing the manifold under the unity of a judging consciousness] (CPR, B 135, p. 154).

This relation between what is given through sensibility and our judging under certain forms of what is given is only possible through epistemic concepts that set up or define the relation:

> All the manifold therefore, so far as it is given in a single empirical intuition, is *determined* in respect of one of the logical functions of judgment, and is thereby brought into one consciousness. Now the *categories* are just these functions of judgment in so far as they are employed in determination of the manifold of a given intuition (CPR, B 143, p. 160).

We saw in connection with the Metaphysical Deduction that *a*) epistemic concepts are concepts that can apply to what is given only insofar as what is given is brought under a certain judgment form. In the Transcendental Deduction it is the converse that is claimed, namely *b*) what is given can be brought under certain forms of judgment only insofar as epistemic concepts apply to what is given. Here *a* shows why epistemic concepts cannot refer merely to what is given through sensible affection; i.e., it shows why epistemic concepts are a priori; and *b* shows why epistemic concepts must be applied to what is given if what is given is to be an object of judgment and if it is to be an object at all; i.e., it shows why epistemic concepts must have objective validity (why they must apply to anything that is to be an object; i.e., an object of judgment) for us. Thus, for example, *a*) the notion of an individual is essentially the notion of a referent of a singular term; i.e., it applies to what is given only insofar as what is given is judged about under the kinds of forms listed under the moment "Of Quantity"; and *b*) we can judge of what is given under quantificational form only if what is given is brought under the concept of an individual.

Hume's failure to understand the possibility of a priori concepts having objective validity is connected with the fact that in a real sense Hume recognizes no problem in how judgment relates to its object. For Hume, the relation of concepts to objects is, we may say, dumb; i.e., it need not be in terms of any rules that set up, e.g., what is to count as one instance of a concept. Concepts are faint images of what is given in sensation. Having a concept, like being sensibly affected, is, for Hume, something that *happens* to the subject (i.e., thinking, like mere sensing, becomes passive). Thinking takes place according to quasimechanical associative laws, not in accordance with intelligent rules. For Hume, there is no problem of how concepts relate to objects; the object is given and simultaneously (or at some later time) the concept (as a faint image) happens to *occur* in the subject.

This failure of Hume's to recognize a problem in the relation of thought to objects goes hand in hand with his failure to understand how a priori modes of knowledge could have objective validity. If thinking is analyzed on the model of sensing, then it is indeed implausible that we could anticipate how we are going to be affected. For example, it is hard to see how we can anticipate how concepts will become associated in our mind in the same way that it is hard to see how we can anticipate how sense qualities should be associated (or collocated) in our experience. As Kant says,

> ... the empirical unity of apperception ... has only subjective validity. To one man, for instance, a certain word suggests one thing, to another some other thing; the unity of consciousness in that which is empirical is not, as regards what is given, necessarily and universally valid (CPR, B 140, p. 158).

I have suggested that the categories are shown to have objective validity in terms of their character as epistemic concepts that set up or define the relation between judgment and its object. This is confirmed, I think, by Kant's discussion of an intuitive understanding, of which he says, "the categories would have no meaning whatsoever in respect of such a mode of knowledge" (CPR, B 145, p. 161). The reason for this is that for an intuitive understanding the very notion of an epistemic concept as dealing with the relation between judgments and objects has no significance. An intuitive understanding is "an understanding . . . through whose representation the objects of the representation should at the same time exist" (CPR, B 139, p. 157), or it is an understanding, "which should not represent to itself given objects, but through whose representation the objects should themselves be given or produced" (CPR, B 145, p. 161). We always distinguish the judgment from what the judgment is about (the object of the judgment). This is true even when our judgment is about concepts. An intuitive understanding would not have this distinction; *the object of judgment would be given "in" the judgment itself.* For example, there would be no distinction between a subject term and what is referred to by a subject term. Having no distinction between judgment and what is judged about, such a subject would make no sense of the idea of an epistemic notion (a notion that relates objects to judgment). It is for this reason that the categories (being epistemic notions) would have no meaning for such a subject.

Up to section 26 in the B-edition Deduction, Kant's discussion of the categories proceeds without specific reference to our forms of intuition, space and time. We shall see in the next section that certain complications are introduced when space and time are specifically brought into the picture and the categories are schematized. For the moment let us remark that the general idea of the relation of judgment to its object makes sense so long as we distinguish judgment from what is given to be judged about, and for this reason the argument can proceed without reference to the specific forms under which what is given is given to us. And yet, as Kant says, "there is one feature from which I could not abstract, the feature, namely, that the manifold to be intuited must be given prior to the synthesis of the understanding and independently of it" (CPR, B 145, p. 161.)

7. The Analogies—The Categories as Conditions of Time-Determination

The central epistemic notion is that of an object of judgment. The object of judgment in experience is that which is given in experience. What is given in experience is given under the forms of space and time. The central epistemic notion for us thus becomes the temporal object of judgment and the central problem becomes, how can something given temporally be an object of judgment? One aspect of this problem is what is to count as an individual object of reference; i.e., what is to count as one object. Quine gives an example to show that what is to count as one object is not determined by sensation, but depends on the subject's conceptualization (viz., in terms of rabbits or rabbit parts). Kant, however, points out a way in which what is to count as an object of reference is not open to alternative conceptualizations on the part of the subject but is determined by sensibility, more specifically by our a priori intuitions of space and time. What Kant points out is that no matter how we divide up what is given sensibly into individuals (i.e., no matter what we take to be the referent of a singular term), what is thus thought of as an individual must have position in a single space and time. Thus, whether we conceptualize what is given in terms of rabbits or rabbit parts, each rabbit (each rabbit part) has some determinate location in space and time.

For Kant, what is conceptualized as an individual must have a determinate position in space and time. This is due to our intuitions regarding the nature of space and time, and what it is for something to be given in space and time. That what is given to us (no matter how it is divided into particular objects) has a position in space and time is something that is not itself due to our conceptualization, or to the possibility of judging about what is given. Our conceptualization of what is to count as an individual (of what is to be a referent of a singular term or a definite description) must conform to this basic aspect of our intuition, namely that whichever way the sensible manifold is "broken up" into individuals, these individuals will have positions in space and time. Thus, judging about what is given will require that we be able to determine what the position of an object (whether a rabbit or a rabbit part or a rabbit stage, or whatever) is in space and time. If there are any concepts in terms of which we must conceptualize what is given in order for us to be able to determine the position of what is given in space and time, these concepts will necessarily have validity with respect to what is given insofar as we are to judge about it. The categories (supposedly) are such concepts.

Despite the foregoing account, the connection between the function of the categories as *i*) conditions of time-determination (in the *Analogies*) and *ii*) as epistemic concepts that bring what is given into line with our forms of judgment (the Metaphysical and Transcendental Deductions), is subject to certain difficulties, difficulties that strike at the heart of the problem of how to read the *Analytic* as the presentation of one continuous argument.

On the one hand the (schematized) relational categories are conditions of judgment because they are conditions of time-determination. On the other hand, the categories are conditions of judgment because they are epistemic concepts corresponding to syntactic forms that make what is given into an object of judgment in accordance with these forms. Now as we have presented it, a crucial aspect of the argument of the Transcendental Deduction is that what is given can be an object of judgment only in terms of certain epistemic categories that connect judgments and what is given. Since these concepts make essential reference to the forms of our judgments (i.e., they only make sense as applying to what is given insofar as we bring in reference to the possibility of our judging about what is given in accordance with certain forms of judgment), such concepts are a priori, that is, not derivable from what is given as such (apart from reference to our forms of judgment). Now the relational categories, as schematized, do not seem to be *epistemic* categories in the sense described at all. Even though the proof of the validity of applying the concept of causality, say, is in terms of the possibility of *judging* about what is given (rather than in terms of merely being sensibly affected as such), this is not sufficient to make causality an epistemic concept; i.e., a concept that has *sense* in relation to what is given only in regard to judging in accordance with certain forms. (For example, the notion of an individual is essentially that of a referent of a singular term; i.e., this notion would not have any sense with regard to what is given except insofar as what is given is judged about in accordance with certain forms [quantification].) It is not that the notion of an individual can only be proven to have objective validity in terms of the possibility of judgment, but that it only has (even purported) sense and significance or meaning in relation to judgment forms. It is not clear that this latter is the case with the schematized concept of causality.

The crux of the transcendental deduction is that it is plausible that a priori concepts should be required for experience since:

> *i*) judgment is essentially involved in experience (in the sense that the subject distinguishes himself from objects primarily by making them objects of his judgment) and;
> *ii*) the relating of judgments to what is given (making

what is given into an object of judgment) cannot itself
be given in experience, but must proceed in terms of certain epistemic (and thus a priori) concepts.

In other words, the transcendental deduction shows that *epistemic*
categories, not derived from what is given as such, are necessary for
experience. *If the argument of the transcendental deduction is to
bear at all on the Analogies—especially stage ii of the argument—
then the schematized relational categories (which are concepts of
time-determination) must, in some sense, retain the character of
being epistemic concepts.*
    It is not at all clear how characterizing a concept as one whose
employment is necessary for time-determination makes that concept
epistemic (even though it is clear, let us grant, from our reconstruction above [pp. 48–49] how so characterizing a concept would make
its employment a necessary condition of judging about what is given).
In other words, concepts whose employment is required for judging
are not ipso facto epistemic concepts. An epistemic concept is not
only a concept that is required if we are to judge about objects, but a
concept that has *meaning* or *significance* with respect to what is
given only insofar as we judge about what is given in accordance
with certain syntactical forms.
    Now a partial solution to this problem is to realize that 'causality',
e.g., may be plausibly construed as an epistemic concept. The clear-
est way I can see this is in terms of Quine's concept of radical translation. We could not determine that the native has a concept of
causality in terms of his responses to sensory stimulation (and our
prompting). We would have to ask the native such questions as,
"*Would* the man have died, if I *had* shot him with an arrow?"
Ultimately, I think only a subject who had a judgment form that
functioned as our counterfactual conditionals could be said to have
and apply a concept of causality. As we shall see in chapter III, the
notion of causality for Kant is one that licenses inferences (Ryle's
inference tickets); it serves as a concept in terms of which we can
infer one fact from another. It is in terms of this aspect that the
concept of causality is distinguished, say, from mere regular succession, and it is this aspect that is (uniquely, I think) indicated by the
acceptance of counterfactual conditionals. If this is true, then the
concept of causality is an epistemic notion in that it only makes sense
insofar as one of our judgment forms is the counterfactual (the non-

material) conditional (hypothetical). Since the concept of causality is, in this sense, an epistemic concept, the argument of the transcendental deduction to this extent would apply.

There remains, however, the following difficulty. A justification or deduction of the concept of causality, if carried out along the lines of the argument of the transcendental deduction, would be that in order to judge in accordance with the hypothetical form of judgment (where the hypothetical is, here, more than the material conditional) we must employ (or is ipso facto to employ) the epistemic concept of causality. Yet in the Analogies the deduction of the concept of causality is that its employment is required for determining succession in time. Why is a different sort of justification offered in the Analogies? The answer I want to offer was suggested to me by the following remark of Bennett's. "The point is that the three categories whose apriority is determinedly argued for in the 'Principles' chapter are the three which most need such argument; their indispensability has not the faintest appearance of following from the table of judgments because they simply do not correspond to the table of judgments as Kant says they do" (Bennett, 1966, p. 93). First, let me point out why I think Bennett's solution will not do. If the relational categories are disassociated or dissevered from the logical functions of judgment (as in Bennett's proposed solution), then they lose their epistemic character (i.e., their character as concepts that apply to what is given only insofar as what is given is brought under certain judgment forms). But this epistemic character is essential if the argument of the Transcendental Deduction is to bear on the Analogies, the argument, i.e., that certain epistemic concepts are required if judgment (and thus experience as distinguished from mere sensible affection) is to be possible.

Now the reason Kant might give a new proof for causality, say, is not that causality does not correspond to the (nonmaterial) hypothetical form of judgment (on the contrary, as I have indicated above, this correspondence is quite plausible—see also pp. 55–57, below), but rather that the nonmaterial hypothetical form of judgment itself does not seem to be a form inextricably bound up with the idea of a being who judges. It would be hard to understand a being who judged and yet whose judgments did not come under quantificational form or something analogous to quantificational form (i.e., whose judgments had no syntactical structure indicating reference to individual [and thus countable] items). It would not, I think (at least prima facie) be incomprehensible to think of a being who judged and yet did not judge under the nonmaterial hypothetical form (i.e., who did not have any subjunctive conditional). The nonmaterial hypothetical is not as central a form of judgment as the forms, say, coming under the heading "Of Quality" and "Of Quantity" (Bennett, 1963, pp. 72, 93). It is this fact, I suggest, that ought to be attributed to Kant as a motivation for offering a new principle for the proof of causality (in terms of time-determination) in the Analogies. A subject who judges about what is given temporally must be able to determine the temporal position of what he is judging about. Therefore, he must employ the concept of causality and *hence one of his forms of judgment must be the nonmaterial hypothetical* (since only as judging under this form can he be said to have and apply the concept of causality). The virtue of this interpretation (which makes the primary worry that of why a being who judges must judge under the nonmaterial hypothetical form) over Bennett's (which makes the primary worry that of why a being who judges under the hypothetical form must have and apply the concept of causality) is that according to this interpretation the *epistemic* nature of the concept of causality need not be given up (and thus the general argument of the transcendental deduction remains relevant).

Let us review our interpretation of the connection of the different sections of the analytic:

1) The Metaphysical Deduction shows that

> *a*) certain concepts applying to objects (rather than to judgments) are *epistemic* concepts; i.e., concepts that correspond to logical forms of judgment in the sense that they are concepts of what is given insofar as what is given is to be brought under these forms of judgment (they have no sense and significance except in relation to judging according to these forms of judgment);
>
> *b*) epistemic concepts, not being concepts of what is given as such but going beyond what is given as referring to our forms of judgment, are a priori.

2) The Transcendental Deduction shows that

> *a*) if experience is to be possible in a sense in which the subject distinguishes himself from what is given to

him, then the subject must make what is given to him into an object of judgment;

b) what is given can be an object of judgment for the subject only if he employs epistemic concepts, which are concepts applying to what is given, enabling him to judge about what is given under certain forms (his forms of judgment).

Let us see how this reconstruction would work for the concept of causality:

Proof A

i) A being who judges about what is given must do so under the nonmaterial hypothetical form of judgment (since this is just one of our forms of judgment).

ii) Thus, by 2b, he must apply the concept of causality to what is given to him.

iii) Hence, if he is to judge about what is given (and thus, by 2a, if he is to have experience), he must apply the concept of causality.

iv) By 1a and 1b, the concept of causality, *qua* being an epistemic concept, cannot be abstracted merely from sensible affection and thus is an a priori concept.

We have argued that it is the weakness of step *i* in Proof A—not any weakness in the transition from *i* to *ii*—that should serve as the imputed reason that in the Analogies Kant gives a new deduction of the concept of causality.

Proof B

i′) A being who judges about what is given temporally must be able to determine (generally) the position in time of what is given to him.

ii′) Employing the concept of causality (i.e., by 1a bringing what is given under the judgment form of the nonmaterial hypothetical) is a condition of time-determination. Thus, by 1′ it is a condition of judging and thus, by 2a, it is a condition of experience.

iii′) Again, by 1a and 1b the concept of causality, qua

being an epistemic concept, cannot be abstracted merely from the sensibly given and so is a priori.

In Proof A, we must judge under the hypothetical form simply because it is one of our forms of judgment. In Proof B we must judge under the nonmaterial hypothetical form because employing the concept of causality is a condition of time-determination, and employing this concept is, ipso facto, to judge in terms of this hypothetical form; i.e., Proof B gives a reason why this form of judgment is indispensable.

Both Proof A and Proof B depend on the correlation of the concept of causality with the nonmaterial hypothetical form of judgment. We must be clear as to exactly what is involved in this correlation. First, it is not the case that a) the nonmaterial hypothetical always is used to make an assertion of causality. "If I were you, I'd be careful" is an injunction to be cautious; it is not even an assertion at all. This, in itself, however, is no objection to the correlation of causality with the nonmaterial hypothetical. What this correlation requires is that *1*) a subject could not judge under the nonmaterial hypothetical form unless he applied the concept of causality. But 1) is not equivalent to 2) every time a subject judges under this form he is asserting a causal connection. Rather, 1) is closer to 3): the whole enterprise ("language-game") of making nonmaterial hypothetical judgments depends in a general way on having and applying the concept of causality. If we could show that the primary use of making nonmaterial hypothetical judgments is to assert causal connections, and other uses of this form can be traced back or seen to be connected to this primary use (or seen to diverge from it in intelligible ways), this would be sufficient for 3) and 1).

Second it is not the case that *b*) every assertion is causality is via the nonmaterial hypothetical judgment. Bennett says, "For one thing causal judgments are as closely allied to universal as to hypothetical judgments." (1963, p. 92). Now I do not deny that a subject *(who has a counterfactual conditional form)* can assert a causal connection by means of a universal judgment. What I wish to maintain, however, is that a subject who had no counterfactual form could not be said to have and apply the concept of causality. The universal form of judgment is not sufficient for a subject applying the concept of causality except insofar as he would "back up" his judgment with counterfactual conditionals, for the universal form itself does not distinguish between accidental and genuinely causal generalizations. This is, I think, peculiarly the function of counterfactual conditionals (the nonmaterial hypothetical). This would be enough to show $1'$ a subject could not apply the concept of causality to what is given except insofar as he could judge under the nonmaterial hypothetical. Thus 1 and $1'$ are what is intended by the correlation of the concept of causality with the nonmaterial hypothetical judgment form, not a and b.

That Kant, in the Analogies, does not give up the connection between the relational categories and the corresponding judgment forms is indicated by part of his explanation of why he uses the term 'analogy'. He says, "By these principles, then, we are justified in combining appearances only according to what is no more than an analogy with the logical and universal unity of concepts" (CPR, A 181, B 224, p. 212). This means, I suggest, that the epistemic concept of, say, causality is applicable only in terms of (on an analogy with) the syntactical relation of antecedent-consequent in the hypothetical judgment form. To say that x and y are causally connected is to say that x and y are brought under the hypothetical form of judgment; i.e., that the terms referring to x and y are syntactically connected in this way. Causality is not an independently characterizable relation to which the syntactic relation of antecedent-consequent corresponds; rather, it is first "introduced" by the use of this syntactic relation.*

Kemp Smith objects that this explanation (let us call it explanation 2) of the term 'analogy' "would involve adoption of the subjectivist standpoint . . . For it implies that it is only in the noumenal and not also in the phenomenal sphere, that . . . genuinely dynamical activities are to be found" (Kemp Smith, 1918, pp. 357–58; see also pp. 373–74). This objection is wrong in two ways. First, the suggested explanation is not that causality holds in the phenomenal sphere only on an analogy with its holding in the noumenal sphere, but rather only on an analogy with the syntactical structure of judgments. Second, to say this is not to say that "dynamical activities" do not "really" hold in the phenomenal sphere; it is to say that categorical concepts, by their very nature, do not apply in the way that empirical concepts do (i.e., it is to give an analysis of what it is for such concepts to "really" apply).

---

* See the passage of Riel's quoted in Kemp Smith, 1918, p. 357.

Kemp Smith further argues that "This interpretation of the term analogy is probably, therefore, of the nature of an afterthought" (Kemp Smith, 1918, p. 357) to the proper explanation (explanation 1) in which the analogy is that some (unknown) *b* is to a given *a* as cause is to effect, where this analogy expresses a rule "according to which a unity of experience a unity of time determination may arise from perception" (CPR, A 180, B 223, p. 211). We shall see in section 18 the way in which the unity of time-determination is bound up with the connection of causality to the hypothetical form of judgment, so that explanation 2 is not in the nature of an afterthought to explanation 1.

The First Analogy

8. *The Argument from Time Magnitude*

"These, then, are the three analogies of experience. They are simply principles of the determination of the existence of appearances in time, according to all its three modes, viz., the relation to time itself as a magnitude (the magnitude of existence, that is, *duration*), the relation to time as a *successive* series, and finally the relation in time as a sum of all *simultaneous* existence" (CPR, A 215, B 262, p. 236). The First Analogy is concerned with the general possibility of determining time magnitude; i.e., determining the lapse of time between events, and determining how long an object remains in a certain state.

I will give a brief outline indicating the results of this section:

> A. Time-determination is only possible in virtue of some feature of appearances, not in virtue of the perception of empty time. This applies to all three modes of time-determination.

> B. The time-determination investigated in the first Analogy, the determination of the magnitude of time intervals, is presupposed in determining succession and coexistence.

> C. A corollary of A is that the determination of time magnitude is only possible in virtue of what is to be found in appearances. Without prejudging what this feature of appearances is, we say that x is the *substratum* of the determination of time magnitude if and only if x is that aspect of appearances in virtue of which we determine the magnitude of time intervals.

   D. Kant's notion of what a substance is is investigated.

   E. I argue that the substrata of the determination of time magnitude are substances and that substances, qua such substrata, must be permanent; i.e., they cannot come into or go out of existence.

   F. I argue (against Kant) that it is compatible with E that no substance in the field of appearance is absolutely permanent.

   G. I argue (against Kant) that though all succession must be determined with respect to substance, this does not imply that all succession is alteration.

A. "All appearances are in time; and in it alone as substratum (as *permanent* form of inner intuition) can either coexistence or succession be represented [italics mine]")CPR, B 225, p. 213). Time is a universal form of intuition in the sense that what is given in experience (everything that is given in experience) is given temporally. That time is the permanent form of intuition is (or at least can be considered) a stronger claim than that time is the universal form of intuition. That time is the permanent form of intuition means not only that everything is given to us temporally, but that the time in which appearances are given to us remains the same. Suppose I perceive x as before y, and then perceive z as before w. Time as a universal form of intuition would only require that "within" each perceptual state objects are given as temporal. Time as a permanent form of intuition would further require that the time in which x precedes y is part of the same time as the time in which z precedes w. Kant says, "Thus the time in which all change of appearances has to be thought remains and does not change" (CPR, B 225, p. 213).
   "Now time by itself cannot be perceived. Consequently, there must be found in the objects of perception, that is, in the appearances, the substratum that represents time in general, and all change or coexistence must in being apprehended be perceived in this substratum, and through relation of appearances to it." If I perceive that x follows y and then perceive that z follows w, I have the "pre-intuition" that the time in which x precedes y and in which z precedes w are two parts of one time, but this pre-intuition gives me no way of determining the actual relation of the two times (which preceded which). Kant's point is that I cannot determine this relation in

virtue of the quality, so to speak, of the two times by themselves. There is nothing about two parts of time by themselves that distinguishes one of them as before, say, the other. Determining the relation of different parts of time is not something that I can do by perceiving these parts by themselves (apart from the occupants). I determine that the time in which z happens, say, is prior to the time in which w happens, based on what z and w are like, not based on what the times that they are in are like. Time by itself is homogeneous; though the parts of time are numerically distinct in virtue of their being located "outside" each other in the single time, there is nothing internal (monadic) about the parts of time by themselves (even if we could perceive the parts of time by themselves; apart from their occupants) that determines what their specific relation is to other parts of time.

B. The First Analogy is concerned with the determination of time magnitude; i.e., with determining (measuring) time intervals. This determination is presupposed in the determination of appearances as successive. Suppose a and b are two terms of a succession (a = ship at place p, b = ship at place p'). No matter what the order of a and b is, that is, no matter whether b succeeds a or a succeeds b, we must be able to determine the temporal interval between a and b. Suppose, for example, that a does precede b. This determination of the relative order of a and b is not sufficient to determine the relative position of a and b in time. The relative position of a and b in time depends also on the time interval between the a obtaining and b obtaining. Thus, if the interval between a and b is three seconds, the relative position of a and b ("where" a and b are with respect to one another in time) is different than if the interval between a and b is three days. It does not make sense (intuitively) to say that a precedes b and yet that the interval between a and b is completely indeterminable. It may be that the interval between a and b is vanishing, but this too must be determinable.

Further, the determination of time magnitude is presupposed in determining the coming to be or ceasing to be of any state of affairs. If a comes to be, it must come to be or begin to exist at some time t', and it must be the case that it did not exist (or obtain) at some time t previous to t'. "If we assume that something absolutely begins to be, we must have a point of time in which it was not" (CPR, A 188, B 231, p. 217). Now, t to t' must constitute some definite time interval. If it began to rain at t' there must be some definite time interval (some magnitude of time) at which it was not raining. Of course, to determine that it began to rain at t', I do not have to determine how long before t' it was not raining. What is required is that it be determinable that there is some time interval up to t' at which it was not raining. Otherwise, how could we say that we have determined that it *began* (rather than *continued*) to rain at t'? There are, of course, "vague" beginnings. A person does not begin to grow senile, perhaps, at a definite, specifiable point of time. We may say that in the last few months x *has begun* to grow senile. Even in this case of vague beginnings (when the coming to be lasts through a time interval, as opposed to coming to be at a point of time), there must be some definite time interval at which x was not growing senile. Otherwise there would be no difference in saying "In the last few months x has begun to grow senile" *versus* "In the last few months x has continued to grow senile."

C. We cannot determine the magnitude of time intervals by perceiving empty time. We cannot determine how long before b event a occurred by perceiving the length of an empty interval between them. Empty time is not something that is marked out with a measure. If we are to determine the time interval between a and b then, as in all determinations of extensive magnitude, it must be in terms of some unit. Metaphorically, time is like a blank sheet of paper as opposed to a sheet of paper ruled with lines where the distance between two adjacent lines mark out the unit of measurement. The actual measure of time must be found in appearances, though the fact that time is amenable to measurement (i.e., that time is an extensive magnitude) derives from intuition.

I make the following distinction that is essential to what follows. That in appearances in terms of which we determine the magnitude of a time interval is, by definition, the *substratum* of the determination of the magnitude of that interval. Thus, the substratum is defined functionally (as that in virtue of which time magnitude is determined), and it is defined relative to the interval that it serves to determine. Different time intervals may be determined in terms of different features of appearances (or, better, in terms of different appearances that possess the relevant feature). Thus, we may measure the time interval between event a and event b in terms of the relative motion of the sun and the earth. We may determine the time interval between event *c* and event *d* in terms of the decay of some radioactive element. The relative motion of the earth and the sun and the decay of the radioactive element are two substrata of the determination of time magnitude, but the relative motion of the earth and the sun, e.g., is *not* a substratum of the determination of the time magnitude between event *c* and event *d*.

According to Kant, there are certain aspects required of anything that is to serve as a substratum of the determination of the magnitude of some time interval. The relevant aspects can be summed up by saying that only substances in the field of appearances can be substrata of the determination of time magnitude. A substance is not defined as that which can serve as a substratum for the determination of time magnitude. Rather, it is defined in terms of permanence. "Certainly, the proposition that substance is permanent is tautological. For this permanence is our sole ground for applying the category of substance to appearance . . ." (CPR, A 184, B 227, pp. 214–15). That substances are what can serve as substrata of time-determination is a synthetic claim. If we can show that only substances (the permanent in appearance) can serve as substrata, we will have shown that substances are required for the determination of time magnitude (and thus that the application of the category of substance is required for any time determination—see B, above p. 60), But this is something that must be shown; i.e., substance is not defined as that which can (only) serve as a substratum of the determination of time magnitude. Kant says, "(1) . . . there must be found in appearances, the substratum that represents time in general. . . . (2) But the substratum of all that is real, that is, of all that belongs to the existence of things, is *substance* . . ." (CPR, B 225, p. 213). Point 2 should not be taken as being a definition of substance. It is rather the claim that only substances in the field of appearance can serve as substrata of time-determination. The conceptual distinction between a substance and a substratum must be kept clearly in mind. We shall see that Kant argues that what is employed as a substratum of determination of time magnitude must be a substance. Yet it is not true that what is a substance is ipso facto employed as a substratum of time-determination.

D. Kant talks of substance as that in appearances whose quantity remains fixed, although this is not a definition of substance. It is a "property" or "characteristic" that Kant argues (mistakenly, I think) that substances must have if they are to be substrata for the determination of time magnitude. Kant's primary motion is that substance, in the field of appearance, is the permanent.

Kant says, in an important passage at the end of the First Analogy, "We shall have occasion in what follows to make such observations as may seem necessary in regard to the empirical criterion of this necessary permanence—the criterion, consequently, of the substantiality of appearances" (CPR, A 189, B 232, p. 217). This criterion of substantiality or permanence turns out to be action. "But I must not leave unconsidered the empirical criterion of a substance in so far as substance appears to manifest itself not through permanence of appearance, but more adequately and easily through action" (CPR, A 204, B 249, pp. 228–29). Again, Kant says, "We are acquainted with substances in space only through forces which are active in this and that space, either bringing other objects to it (attraction) or preventing them penetrating into it (repulsion and impenetrability)" (CPR, A 265, B 321, p. 279). By action, Kant seems to be referring to a nexus of causality (and dynamical community). Space and its occupants contain only formal and real relations. Real relations, such as the dynamical actions of phenomena upon each other, are coordinated with formal relations (relative positions in space) to give rise to the idea of objects as centers of action. That the real relations are coordinated with the formal relations means that different dynamical centers of action are identifiable as located (or concentrated) in different regions of space, and that changes in dynamical action correlate with changes in spatial position. For example, the dynamical action of the sun on other phenomena is a function of the spatial position of the sun with respect to these other phenomena. The sun and the earth are distinguished as different substances by their different interactions with still other phenomena in space. The dynamical interaction of the sun and the moon is different from the dynamical action of the earth and the moon (the sun is subject to or part of different sets of interactions than the earth), and this difference is correlated with the difference in spatial position of the sun and the earth (the sun is a spatial nexus of a different set of interactions than the set of which the earth is a spatial nexus). "All that we know in matter is merely relations . . . but among these relations some are self-subsistent and permanent, and through these we are given a determinate object" (CPR, A 285, B 341, p. 291).

What relation is there between the following two claims, both of which seem central to Kant's theory of substance?

1) Only substance (the permanent in appearances) can serve as a substratum of the determination of time magnitude.

2) Action is the empirical criterion of substance.

Now, it seems plausible to say that we determine the magnitude of time intervals in terms of certain actions (like the mechanism of an ordinary face-clock). Something permanent in appearance that does not change at all, can no more serve to determine time magnitude than empty time itself. Kant says, ". . . we must derive the determination of lengths of time from the *changes* which are exhibited to us in outer things [italics mine]" (CPR, B 156, p. 268). The connection between 1 and 2 seems to be the following: *Only if we take action as a criterion of substance can action serve as a basis for the determination of time magnitude.* In other words, only if actions are taken to be actions of what persists through the action can we determine time magnitude on the basis of action. Only insofar as we consider a series of states of affairs as alterations of a persistent thing does this series become an appropriate means of time measurement. Claim (3), Only substance (the permanent) can be a substratum for the determination of the magnitude of time, is to be analyzed as Claim (4), Only if we take an action to be the action of a thing that persists through a certain time interval (this is, only if action is a criterion of substance) can that action be used to determine the magnitude of that time interval. Claim 4 sums up the relationship between claims 1 and 2. We argue for claim 4 in E.

E. We first discuss what is involved in an object's persisting through (or having permanence in) a time interval (I). We then argue for a modified version of claim 4 of D (II).

I. One way to get at what is involved in an object persisting through a time interval is to see how an object can fail to persist through an interval. One philosophically important way it can fail is the following. I perceive A at time t and then percenve A′ at time t′, where A and A′ are qualitatively identical. If A exists only so long as I perceive it, and A′ exists only so long as I perceive it, then during an interruption of my perception neither A nor A′ exists. Thus, neither A nor A′ persisted through the time interval t to t′. Now, philosophers concerned with how we can know that an object persists during an interval that includes an interruption in our perception usually take it to be clear enough what it is for an object to persist during an interval of uninterrupted perception. Hume, for example, asks what makes us believe that A and A′ are the same object? His answer is that the disposition of the imagination in the case of the interrupted perception is the same as the disposition of the imagination during an interval of uninterrupted perception (Hume, 1888, pp 202–4). I can, according to Hume, perceive an object that persists through that interval (of uninterrupted perception). He says, "Thus the principle of individuation is nothing but the *invariableness* and *uninterruptedness* of any object thro' a supposed variation of time, by which the mind can trace it in the different periods of its existence, without any break of the view, and without being oblig'd to form the idea of multiplicity or number" (Hume, 1888, p. 201). Thus, for Hume, it is sufficient for A at t and A′ at t′ to be two "stages" (states) of one object that persists through the time interval t to t′, if at all times t_x between t and t′ there exists A_x at t_x such that A_x is qualitatively identical to A (and A′). This condition is, of course, not usually taken to be necessary, for objects may persist through an interval in which they undergo qualitative change. The *invariableness* is that all the A_x are qualitatively identical; the uninterruptedness is that there is no time t_x between t and t′ at which some A_x does not exist. It seems clear that invariableness and uninterruptedness are necessary conditions of the persistence of qualitatively unchanging objects through time. It may not seem clear that these conditions are sufficient. Are A and A′ two stages of one persisting object or are A and A′ two different objects mediated by a series of *continuous* replacements in which there is no lacuna? The simplest case would be where there is just one replacement. Certainly, if A went out of existence at time t_x and A′ came into existence at time t_y (with no A_z existing between t_x and t_y), then no matter how small the interval between t_x and t_y, it would make sense to say that no object persisted through any interval that encompasses the interval from t_x to t_y. But does it make sense to say that A lasted from t to t_x and A′ lasted from t_y to t′, where $t_x = t_y$ (i.e., at the precise time A went out of existence, A′ came into existence), and yet that no object persisted (filled the time) during the entire interval t to t′? I shall assume that it does not make sense and take it that *uninterruptedness* in the sense just explained is the relevant sense of the permanence or persistence of a thing through a time interval. Claim 4 of D now becomes

(4′) Only if we take an action to be the action of a thing that is uninterrupted (though not invariable, for the thing may undergo change) in its existence during a certain time interval can that action be used to determine the magnitude of that time interval.

II. Suppose that the action (mechanism) of an ordinary face-clock is used to determine the magnitude of a time interval t_1 to t_2. We assume that at time t_1 the hands on the clock read 4:00 A.M. and that at time t_2 the hands on the clock read 4:05 A.M. We thus measure the time interval t_1 to t_2 as the time it takes for the action (the mechanism) to move the hands of the clock from a 4:00 reading to a 4:05 reading. Suppose that the clock that reads 4:00 at t_1 does not have an uninterrupted existence up to time t_2; i.e., suppose we have the following situation: At time t_1 clock A reads 4:00. At time $t′$ between t_1 and t_2 clock A goes out of existence. At some time $t″$ between $t′$ and t_2 (where $t″$ does not equal $t′$) clock B comes into existence and at t_2 clock B reads 4:05. In order to determine the time interval between t_1 and t_2 we must be able to determine the interval between $t′$ and $t″$. It will not do in determining this interval to say, e.g., that since the last reading of clock A (at $t′$) was 4:02.25, and the first reading of clock B (at $t″$) was 4:02.27, that the interval $t′$ to $t″$ was 2 seconds. For the face readings of the clocks are only significant as the results (the effects) of the mechanical actions of the two clocks. The significance of B reading 4:02.27 vis-à-vis A reading 4:02.25 is lost, since it is not coordinated with any action during the interval $t′$ to $t″$. The time between $t′$ and $t″$ is not marked off by the mechanical process.

Thus, there can be no interval no matter how small (because we could not determine how small) between the times t_1 and t_2 at which there is a lacuna in the mechanism, if this mechanism is to be that in virtue of which we determine the magnitude of the interval t_1 to t_2. There can be no interruption during the interval t_1 to t_2 of the thing acting that serves as the substratum of the determination of the magnitude of the interval between t_1 and t_2. In other words, the spring or the pendulum that acts cannot go out of existence at time $t′$ and be replaced by another spring or pendulum at $t″$ if $t′$ does not equal $t″$. We said in part E-I that unless there were such a time interval between t and $t′$, then the spring or pendulum is to be considered as persisting (uninterrupted) in its existence, and thus claim 4′ follows.

It is clear now that if we are to determine the time interval be-tween our perceptions, then we must consider some substance as per-sisting through the time interval of the interruption; i.e., as persist-ing through the time when we are not perceiving it.

F. It does not follow from 4′ that 5) substances cannot go out of existence or come into existence. All that follows is that substances, employed as substrata, cannot come into existence or go out of exis-tence during the time intervals for which they serve as such a sub-stratum of the determination of time magnitude. Claim 5 would only follow from 4′ if we could establish something like the follow-ing: 6) If a substance is employed as a substratum for the determina-tion of the magnitude of any time interval, then that substance is (or ought to be) employed as a substratum for the determination of the magnitude of *all* time intervals. From claim 6 it would follow that something in appearances must be absolutely permanent (i.e., lasting throughout all time).

What reason could there be for holding claim 6? Kant says, "Sub-stances in the (field of) appearance, are the substrata of all deter-mination of time. If some of these substances could come into being and others cease to be, the one condition of the empirical unity of time would be removed" (CPR, A 188, B 231, p. 217). Or he says, ". . . the unity of experience would never be possible if we were willing to allow that new things, that is, new *substances* could come into existence. For we should then lose that which alone can repre-sent the unity of time, namely the identity of the substratum wherein alone all change has thoroughgoing unity" (CPR, A 186, B 229, p. 216). Is it a condition of the empirical unity of time that new *sub-strata* cannot come into being; i.e., that we cannot employ a previ-ously unemployed substance as a substratum for the determination of time magnitude? Suppose we determine the magnitude of the in-terval between events E_1 and E_2 in terms of some acting substance A, which persists through (at least) that interval and the interval between events F_1 and F_2 in terms of B acting, as shown in Fig. 1.

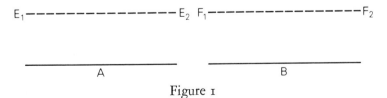

E_1 ---------------E_2 F_1 ---------------F_2

A   B

Figure 1

Then we shall have no way of determining the interval between E_2 and F_1, say, and thus the empirical unity of time would be lost. Consider, however, the situation in Fig. 2.

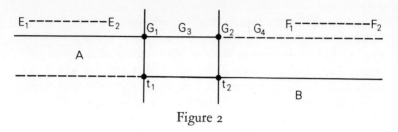

Figure 2

We use A as the substratum up to time t_2, and B as the substratum after t_2. During the interval t_1 to t_2 the action of B is correlated with the action of A. Suppose A is the motion of a pendulum and B is the position of the earth in its orbit around the sun. The correlation of B with A would involve, say, if the earth moves x miles in the time it takes the pendulum to complete y movements, then the earth moves nx miles in the time it takes the pendulum to complete ny movements. It seems that in this way the interval between E_2 and F_1 can be determined by adding the interval between E_2 and G_2 (as determined by A) to the interval between G_2 and F_1 (as determined by B). One may argue that there is an important empirical assumption involved, namely, that the action of B continues to correlate with the action of A after time t_2, for otherwise (apparently) the interval between E_2 and F_1 could not be unambiguously determined. Suppose, for example, that the pendulum completes x movements from G_2 to G_4 and x movements from G_4 to F_1, but that the earth moves y miles between the times of G_2 and G_4 and 2y miles between the times of G_4 and F_1. Then the interval (G_4, F_1) is equal to or twice as great as the interval (G_2, G_4) depending on whether it is determined by A or B. In such a situation, any intervals encompassing the interval between G_2 and F_1 would also be ambiguous. "The appearances would then relate to two different times, and existence would flow in two parallel streams—which is absurd" (CPR, A 189, B 232, p. 217).

The source of the difficulty here is not that we have given up A as a substratum in favor of B, but that we use B as a substratum *without* having given up A as a substratum. If we use the actions of two different substances both as substrata for the determination of the magnitude of the same time interval, then there is always the possibility of two conflicting determinations of the magnitude of this interval. If, however, we give up the action of A *as a substratum,* then no conflict or ambiguity is possible, for the intervals are then determined solely in terms of B. In the situation described above we would simply say that the pendulum is moving half as fast during the interval G_4 to F_1 as it was during the interval G_2 to G_4. If we are using B as the substratum for the interval G_2 to F_1, then we *must* decide that the action of the pendulum has slowed down rather than that the motion of the earth has speeded up. The point is, there is no a priori reason for saying that we ought never to give up A in favor of B as the substratum of time-determination, for there may be excellent empirical reasons for abandoning A. For example, if the pendulum is strongly magnetic and is transferred to a region with an erratically varying magnetic field, we would give up the motion of the pendulum as a measure of time intervals. In other words, that the action of A is used as a substratum for the determination of time magnitude does not mean that A must (or ought) always be employed as such a substratum. The empirical unity of time, in certain cases, may be better served by abandoning the use of A as a substratum for the determination of the magnitude of time intervals.

G. Nor does it follow from 4′ that all succession is alteration. It is analytic that alterations are changes of state of substances, for "Alteration is a way of existing which follows upon another way of existing of the same object" (CPR, A 187, B 320, p. 216). It is a synthetic claim, however, that all change in the field of appearance is alteration.

Kant says, "If we assume that something absolutely begins to be, we must have a point in time at which it was not. But to what are we to attach this point if not to that which already exists? For a preceding empty time is not an object of perception."[1] We can only think of x as coming into being by thinking of it as coming into being at some time. This implies that there is a time at which x was not. Further, there must be some definite period of time at which x was not (see B, above, p. 60). Now we cannot by reference to empty time determine a time interval at which x was not. We can only determine a time interval at which x was not in terms of some substratum for the determination of time intervals; i.e., in terms of the action of some substance that exists through some interval at which x was not *and persists up to the time of the coming to be of x.* For suppose we think of x as coming to be at time t2 and that A (the substratum) persists from t0 to t1 where t1 is prior to t2. If A ceases to be before t2, the question arises, how much before? If we cannot determine how much before, then we have not determined at what point x comes into being. (The time of the coming to be of x must at least be determinable with respect to the time of the ceasing to be of A.) How are we to determine the time magnitude between the coming to be of x and the ceasing to be of A? Only in terms of some B that persists at least during the interval from the ceasing to be of A to the coming to be of x. But then B is a substratum that persists during a time interval at which x was not and up to the time of the coming to be of x.

Thus, we must "connect the coming to be with things which previously existed and which persist in existence up to the moment of this coming to be" (CPR, A 187, B 320, p. 216). Kant goes on to conclude from this that "this latter [that which comes to be] must simply be a determination of what is permanent in that which precedes it" (CPR, A 184, B 227, p. 214). That the coming to be of x can only be determined (ascertained) in relation to some substance B that exists before and up to the coming to be of x does not imply that x is a determination (accident or state) of B. It does not follow that since the coming to be of x is determined with respect to B that the coming to be of x is the coming to be of a state of B; i.e., that the coming to be of x is an alteration in B.

Suppose we have a succession *a-b*. We must be able to determine the magnitude of the time interval between *a* and *b*. If I determine the magnitude of the time interval between *a* and *b* in terms, say, of the motion of the earth in its orbit about the sun, it does not follow that *a* and *b* are determinations (accidents) of the earth or the sun or, for that matter, of any substance at all that persists through the time interval of the succession. From the fact that "the permanent in appearances is therefore the substratum of all determination of time" (CPR, A 188, B 231, p. 217), it does not follow that "All existence and all change have thus to be viewed simply as a mode of the existence of that which remains" (CPR, A 184, B 227, p. 214).

Note, I do not wish to deny claim *a*) that only states of substances, not substances themselves, come to be or cease to be. What I have wished to deny is that this claim follows from the conception of substances as the substrata of the determination of time magnitude, and the resulting fact that no coming to be or ceasing to be can be determined in time except by reference to some substance. It seems that Kant is committed to the following:

1) It is not self-contradictory to deny claim *a*).

2) The justification of claim a does not depend at all on whether or not we can *imagine* (or conceive) substances to come into or go out of existence, in the sense that the justification of the claim that two straight lines do not enclose a space does depend on what we can imagine or intuitively grasp. Claim *a*) is not intuitively justifiable because it is a *dynamical* rather than a mathematical claim. Hence, claim a must be justified on the basis of its relevance to time-determination. This can be attempted either directly or indirectly. A direct justification would show that we could not determine that x came to be, e.g., unless x were the coming to be of a state of some substance. An indirect justification would show that causality and interaction are required for time-determination, and that these, in turn, in some way presuppose that substances do not come into or go out of existence. A direct justification of claim a on the basis of the function of substances as substrata for the determination of time magnitude is, I have been arguing, unpromising. In section 9 I indicate, with excessive brevity, another line of thought that would supply a direct justification.

9. The Argument from Empirical Verifiability

Kant says (at A 188, B 231, p. 217):

> Alteration can therefore be perceived only in substances. A coming to be or ceasing to be that is not simply a determination of the permanent but is absolute, can never be a possible perception. For this permanent is what alone makes possible the representation of the transition . . . from not-being to being. These transitions can be empirically known only as changing determinations of that which is permanent.

Suppose we wished to determine that some substance S came into being at time t. Then we would have to determine that S did not exist prior to t, at t′ say (otherwise S just *continues* to be at t). But how are we to empirically determine (verify) that S did not exist at t′? It seems that this would involve determining that for all places p, S did not exist at any p at t′, and this latter does not seem to be empirically determinable in a straightforward way. Suppose, however, that we conceptualize the coming to be as an alteration; i.e., we think of it as some object x coming to be S. Now to empirically determine this, all we would have to do is determine that *a*) x was not S at t′, rather than that *b*) S did not obtain at any place at all at t′; *a* as opposed to *b* does seem to be straightforwardly verifiable (empirically determinable) or, as Kant would say, a "possible perception."

The difference in empirical verifiability between *a* and *b* depends upon and is indicative of a certain conception of what is involved in organizing the empirically given in terms of the notion of substance. Thus *a* is verifiable only because the spatial positions of states of substances are subject to limitations. If the only way we could determine that x was not S at t′ was to scan all of space, find x, and see that it was not S, then *a* would be no more verifiable than *b*. What I wish to suggest in the following remarks is that there is a viable interpretation of the notion of substance that would preclude our having to scan all of space.

The phenomenon of an electron and a positron resulting from a photon is termed *pair creation*. It seems here we have two substances coming into existence. What is the significance of describing this phenomenon as the *creation* of an electron? Part of the answer, it seems, is that there are no laws connecting this electron being here (in a certain vicinity) at this moment with an electron being anywhere else in space at the previous moment. More specifically, it is the lack of *qualitatively similar* ancestor to this electron, connected spatially with this electron via laws, which inclines us to say that this electron is created here rather than that it moved here. Now certainly this electron being *here* is connected via laws to *some* other phenomenon obtaining at a certain time at a certain place; namely, to the localized action of photons, only these photons are qualitatively quite dissimilar from the electron.

What I think Kant needs to say is that spatial law-governedness is a consideration that overrides qualitative similarity. Insofar as this electron being here is connectible via laws with *some* other phenomenon (qualitatively similar or not) occurring at some other (specified) place, the electron coming to be here is to be thought of as a change of substance (from a photon-state to an electron-state).

In other words, to say that a state of affairs S_2 is the state of a substance is to say no more than that the state of affairs S_2 obtaining at a certain place at a certain time is connectible by laws to some other state of affairs S_1 obtaining previously at some other specified place, such that if S_2 had obtained anywhere at the previous time it would have been at that place where S_1 obtained.

Notice that when we conceptualize the coming to be of S_2 as the coming to be of a state of a substance according to the above interpretation of what this conceptualization involves, we limit ipso facto where we have to look to determine that S_2 did not obtain previously. For example, when we think of the electron coming to be as a transition to an electron-state from a photon-state, what we are doing is saying that if this electron-state was *anywhere* at the previous moment, it was there where the photon-state was, and it was there instead of the photon-state. It would be there instead of the photon-state in the sense that if the photon-state had *not* obtained previously, the electron-state would have obtained in the vicinity where the photon-state did obtain. This is what is involved in saying the electron-state is created *from* (or out of) the photon-state, or that the photon-state *becomes* the electron-state. We have only to look at that place where our laws tell us the electron-state had to be if it were anywhere in order to determine whether the electron-state came to be at this time or persisted (i.e., continued to be).

In general terms, to conceptualize states of affairs as states of substances enables us to ascertain empirically when a state of affairs comes to be as opposed to when it persists. What the conceptualization comes down to is the claim (based on some laws relating spatial position) that if the state of affairs obtained anywhere at the previous moment it had to be at a particular place. If this is the claim that is involved essentially in conceptualizing a state of affairs as a state of a substance, then it is comprehensible how the coming to be of states of substances is ascertainable empirically (empirically distinguishable from their *continuing* to be), while the coming to be of states of affairs not considered states of substances is not ascertainable. It is only in the former case that determining S_2 did not obtain anywhere previously reduces to determining that S_2 did not obtain at some particular place previously. It is the notion of substance that effects this reduction.

The same line of argument implies that only *states* of substances go out of existence. If it is to be determinable empirically that a state of affairs S_1 went out of existence at time t, then it must be determinable that S_1 obtains at no place now (i.e., the moment after t). If this is to be possible it will again require some such law as, if S_1 obtains *anywhere* now, it obtains at a certain place (the place where S_2 now obtains), and again it is such a law that is involved in thinking of S_1 as a state of a substance (the substance that is now S_2). For example, we determine that the photon-state went out of existence a moment ago in terms of the conceptualization that if it were anywhere now it would be where the electron-state now obtains.

The question still remains, however, whether substances are permanent. This question is not, I think, answered automatically even if we grant that only states of substances come into or go out of existence. The natural inference to make is that since only *states* of substances come into or go out of existence, substances themselves do not come into or go out of existence, so substances are permanent. But there is the possibility (which I think viable in this case) that the inference is fallacious in the same way as the inference from oranges are not sad to oranges are happy is fallacious. Substances cannot properly be said to come into existence, go out of existence, *or persist*. The class to which the predicates "come into existence," "go out of existence," "persists" are applicable are particular states of affairs, and the notion of substance is not that of a state of affairs.

That the verifiability argument does not prove that substances persist can, I think, be brought out by considering another verifiability argument to the conclusion that only states of substances can be empirically determined to *persist*. In order to determine that a state of affairs S_2 at p_2 at t_2 has persisted (as opposed to it coming to be at t_2), we would have to determine that S_2 was at some p_1 at t_1. Suppose we have determined that a state of affairs S_2^* (in every respect similar to S_2) obtained at p_1 at t_1. This in itself is not evidence that S_2 did not come to be at t_2, unless we can also rule out the possibility that S_2^* is now (at t_2) at some *other* place. If S_2^* is at any other place p_3, then it is that state of affairs at p_3 that has persisted. We must be able to determine that S_2^* is *nowhere* else now. Ultimately this is determinable empirically only in terms of some law implying that if S_2^* is anywhere now, it is where S_2 is now and such a law would (ipso facto) be a conceptualization of S_2 and S_2^*, as constituting a persisting state *of a substance*. Thus, a state of affairs can be determined empirically to have persisted only if it is conceptualized as a state of a substance. Consequently, only states of substances persist. Now if one wanted to say that the conclusion of the original verifiability argument (viz., only states of substances come into or go out of existence) implies that substances persist, it seems that one ought equally to say that the conclusion of the argument of this paragraph (viz., only states of substances persist) implies that substances themselves do not persist.

Let me recapitulate, then, the argument from empirical verifiability:

1) S_1 and S_2 are states of a substance at t_1 and t_2, means by definition that they are connected in the following way. If S_2 had been anywhere at t_1, it would have been where S_1 was at t_1 if S_1 had not been anywhere at t_1.

2) It is determinable that a state of affairs S_2 came into existence at p_2 at t_2 only if it is determinable that S_2 did not obtain anywhere at t_1 (just prior to t_2).

3) It is determinable that S_2 did not obtain anywhere at t_1 only if there is a law implying that if S_2 obtained anywhere at t_1, it could only have obtained where some other state of affairs S_1 obtained.*

4) Thus, it is determinable that S_2 did not obtain anywhere at t_1 only if there is some S_1 such that S_2 and S_1 are connected as states of a substance.

In conclusion, there are two virtues (one relative to Kant and one absolutely) that I wish to suggest for this argument and the associated notion of substance. First, space is as involved in this argument as time. It is the coming to be of states of affairs *in space* to which it pertains. In this sense the argument is in the spirit of Kant's marginal note that the argument of the First Analogy ought to be recast in terms of space (Kemp Smith, 1918, p. 361). It seems clear from the passages quoted at the beginning of this section that Kant had some sort of empirical verifiability argument in mind for the claim that only states of substances begin to be or cease to be. What I have tried to do is show how such an argument might be worked out if space is taken into account. The argument, if successful, does show

---

* It will do no good to say we can determine empirically that 1) S_2 was not in the *vicinity* of p_2 at time t_1 (this does not require us to scan all of space), and that this is evidence that 2) S_2 was nowhere at time t_1. 1 is evidence for 2 only if there is some *law* to the effect that, if S_2 were anywhere at t_1 it was in the vicinity of p_2.

that substantiality is presupposed in all time-determination. Events or happenings are the proper relata of the temporal relations of succession and simultaneity. But we could not determine something as a happening (something coming to be, as opposed to continuing to be) at all unless it was a substance state. It is the notion of a state of substance that enables us to determine something as a proper relatum for time relations.

Second, the notion of substance called forth by this argument is not, I think, too great a departure from our ordinary notion, yet the departure is wide enough to make it plausible to say that science must employ the notion of substance. One way it departs is in the lack of insistence upon qualitative similarity as an essential feature of substance. We usually require that qualitative transitions between states of substances are not drastic. There is a distinction between drastic transition and law—governed transition. The transition from the photon-state to the electron-state is drastic in a sense in which even a transition such as that from wood to ashes is not. In the former case the two states are categorized by two different sets of for the most part nonoverlapping predicates. In the latter case, although the specific quality changes are extreme, they are not changes in kind. The extreme change of color is not a change from one *kind* of categorization to another, but rather an extreme change within the color categorization. Once it is recognized that law-governedness can extend to drastic transitions, the door is opened to a more generalized conception of substance in which qualitative similarity is replaced by lawfulness.*

Another way in which the notion of substance associated with the empirical verifiability argument departs from the ordinary notion is that spatial *continuity* is not held to be essential in the more generalized notion. What is essential is that the spatial position of different states be *law-governed*. What is important is the inference from 1) S_2 is a state of affairs here (P_2), now (t_2), to 2) if S_2 obtained anywhere previously it obtained at a certain place P_1. It is not essen-

---

* There is a kind of predicate attribution more drastic yet than that involved in drastic *transition*. I refer to the duality of particle and wave where nonoverlapping classes of predicates apply *simultaneously* to the same subject. I do not think that this in itself is proof that we are not conceptualizing here in terms of states of substances. Strawson's idea of a person as that to which both M and P predicates are applicable is another instance of this more drastic attribution. I do not think this *in itself* precludes us from thinking of persons as substances.

tial that we be able to infer from this that if S_2 obtains at P_1 at time t_1 and at P_2 at time t_2, then S_2 obtained at all positions along some arc $\widehat{P_1P_2}$ during the interval t_1 to t_2.

Another question arises, namely, what is to be made of this argument when the modern notion of laws as probabilistic in nature is taken into account? Step 3 of the argument says that it is determinable empirically that S_2 did not obtain at any place at t_1, only in terms of some law that states that had S_2 obtained anywhere at t_1, it *could only* (or *must*) *have* obtained where some other state of affairs S_1 obtained. But according to the modern view there are no such laws (or at least no such laws are in our possession). What happens to step 3 when the law only states that had S_2 obtained anywhere at t_1, it *would probably have* obtained (etc.), is that it is no longer determinable *conclusively* that S_2 came into existence (as opposed to persisted) but it is determinable in a nonconclusive sense; i.e., we still would have some evidence or reason for believing that S_2 did not persist. In sum, the conclusion of the argument would be generalized to: If we are to have any evidence for believing that S_2 came to be, we must conceptualize S_2 as a state of a substance, where conceptualizing it as a state of a substance now means bringing S_2 under some law to the effect that if S_2 had been anywhere previously, it *probably* would have been where S_1 was previously and instead of S_1.

Finally, it must be noted that the argument from empirical verifiability itself is not sufficient to establish an important element of Kant's claim in the first Analogy, for the argument only purports to show that all *spatial* coming to be and ceasing to be requires the notion of substance, whereas the claim of the First Analogy extends to the coming to be and ceasing to be of mental states. It is for this reason that some such argument from the determination of time magnitude as presented in the first section of this chapter is required, an argument that shifts the burden to *spatial* states of affairs.

3 *The Second and Third Analogies*

10. *Perception of a Succession*

The fact that I perceive A and B *successively* does not imply that A and B are successive as opposed to coexistent. Yet there is something that we can say about our perceptions of a succession A-B, as opposed to our perceptions of two coexisting items A, B. The distinguishing feature concerns the possibility of reversing the order of our perceptions.

> In the series of these perceptions [of what objectively coexists] there was no determinate order specifying at what point I must begin in order to connect the manifold empirically. But in the perception of an event there is always a rule that makes the order in which the perceptions (in the apprehension of this appearance) follow upon one another a necessary order (CPR, A 193, B 238, p. 221).

If I perceive A and then perceive B, and this succession of perceptions is the perception of a succession A-B, then I could not have first perceived B and then A. Bennett objects to this analysis (1966, pp. 221–28). First, he says that if I in fact first perceived A and then perceived B, then my perception of A must have preceded my perception of B no matter whether A is objectively coexistent with B or A is precedent to B. This, of course, is correct if we are talking about the succession of my perceptions. Granted the succession went one way, it is impossible that that succession of perceptions could have gone the other way and still have been the same succession of perceptions (of events in my mental history), and this is true irrespective of whether the perceptions are of a succession or of what coexists. And yet there is no reason to think that Kant is confused on this point. Bennett's reason for thinking Kant is confused here is based on B 258, A 211 (1966, p. 221). Bennett must be referring to the following passage:

> Things are coexistent so far as they exist in one and the same time. But how do we know that they are in one and the same time? We do so when the order in the synthesis of apprehension of the manifold is a matter of indifference, that is, whether it be from A through B, C, D, to E or, in reverse, from E to A. For if they [A, B, C, D, E] were in succession to one another in time, in the order say which begins with A and ends in E, it is impossible that we should begin the apprehension in the perception of E and proceed backward to A, since A belongs to past time and can no longer be an object of apprehension (CPR, A 211, B 258, p. 234).

It seems clear that Kant is saying here that if things are not coexistent, if *A, B, C, D, E* are successive (not if our perception of A, perception of B, etc., are successive), then it is impossible to first apprehend E, then D, back to A. It seems highly implausible that Kant means here that ". . . if they [my apprehensions] were in succession to one another in time," since *for Kant my apprehensions are always successive.* The qualification, *if* they were in succession, seems evidence that Kant is not talking about the succession of apprehensions, but rather about the succession in what is apprehended.

Bennett is more concerned, I think, to argue his second objection. He gives the following counterexample to Kant's analysis: "(a) I saw a long boat rowed out of the harbor: which if Kant's analysis is right, entails not just that my visual states *did* occur in a certain order but that (b) I *could not have had them in any other order.* But since the coxswain of the boat was under orders from me, I could have secured for myself the spectacle of the boat being back-paddled, stern-foremost, into the harbor. So (a) is true and (b) is false and Kant's analysis of (a) is therefore wrong" (1966, p. 222). Bennett's objection is that if A came before B, I still could have first perceived B and then perceived A by acting (interfering) to make B come before A. Let us call A coming before B *event 1* and B coming before A *event 2* (certainly these are two different events). The fact that if I had perceived event 2, rather than event 1, the order of my perceptions would have been reversed (which is all that Bennett's objection amounts to) does not mitigate against the fact that given I perceived event 1, my perception of A had to precede my perception of B (Bird, 1962, p. 160; Strawson, 1966, pp. 134–35). On the other hand, if I first perceive A, thinking that B also exists at this time, and then perceive B, thinking A continues to exist, this is to think of the same state of affairs as if I had first perceived B thinking A also exists at this time, and then perceived A thinking B continues to exist. Bird says, regarding the apprehension of a succession, "... if the constituent states had been reversed, the event apprehended would have been a different event. It would have been the event of a ship's sailing upstream" (Bird, 1962, p. 155).

If I think of A, B as related successively, and I think of this succession as in the object, then I must think of it as either A following B or B following A. Otherwise the event A-B would not be distinguished from the event B-A. The succession must be *determinate:* i.e., it must be either A-B or B-A, and in either case my successive apprehensions are "bound down" to this order in apprehending the event. "In this case we must derive the *subjective succession* of apprehension from the *objective succession* of appearances" (CPR, A 193, B 238, p. 221).

There are thus two features involved in our apprehension of a succession in appearances: (i) the order of the terms of the succession must be determinate; and (ii) the order of apprehension of the terms of the succession follows the order of the terms of the succession itself. Kant seems to want to conclude that "Therefore since there is certainly something that follows (i.e., is *apprehended* as following) I must refer it necessarily to something else which precedes it and upon which it follows in conformity with a rule, that is, of necessity. The event as the conditioned thus affords reliable evidence of some condition, and this condition is what determines the event" (CPR, A 194, B 239, p. 222). Commentators have taken this conclusion of the Second Analogy as proceeding from i and ii, the crux being ii.

Let us follow Paton's notation and denote by a the perception of α and by b the perception of β. If a subject successively perceives the succession α-β, then the order of his perceptions must be a-b. The succession a-b is causally determined in the following sense: What determines a to precede b is that α precedes β and α is the immediate cause of a and β is the immediate cause of b. From this it does not follow that every succession (α-β) is causally determined. First, it does not even follow that every succession *of percep-tions* is causally determined. All that has been shown is that if the succession of perceptions *a-b* is the perception *of a succession* α-β, then *a* is causally determined to precede *b*. But not every succession of perceptions is the perception of a succession. It has not been shown that if α and β are coexistent then *a* is causally determined to precede *b* (and yet *a-b* is certainly a *succession* of perceptions). Second, not every succession is a succession of perceptions. It has not been shown that α is causally determined to precede β, yet α-β is a succession.

Paton argues that Kant's transition from claim ii to the claim that every succession is causally determined is invalid unless (perhaps) we adopt the "critical principle" that appearances are contents of sense perceptions, not things in themselves. He says, "If the event α and the event β were things in themselves, it is manifest that we could never pass from the common sense assertion that, in perceiving the objective succession α-β, sense perception *a* of α must be followed by sense perception *b* (of β) to the quite different assertion that the objective succession αβ is itself causally determined. Kant appears to be arguing that since the event α and the event β are, on critical principles, only the content of sense perceptions *a,* and *b,* the attribution of necessary succession to *a* and *b* (on the ground of the objectivity of the succession αβ) is ipso facto an attribution of necessary succession to α and β" (Paton, 1936, 2:242, 247, 264). If all that is meant by saying that α and β are contents of sense perceptions *a* and *b* is that α is what is apprehended in perception *a* and β is what is apprehended in perception *b,* then that appearances are contents of sense perceptions does not make the transition any more plausible. We cannot conclude from the fact 1) that *a* is causally determined to precede *b* if what is apprehended in *a* (α) precedes what is apprehended in *b* (β), to the claim 2) that what is apprehended in *a* is causally determined to precede what is apprehended in *b*. On the other hand, if what is meant by saying that α and β are contents of sense perceptions *a* and *b* is that α is to be identified with *a* and β is to be identified with *b* (appearances are perceptual acts, not what is perceived) then, "ipso facto" if *a* is causally determined to precede *b,* α is causally determined to precede β. But now what justification is there for saying that *a* is causally determined to precede *b*? Not that the order of our apprehensions *a-b* is bound down to the order of what is apprehended α-β, for we no longer have two orders (such that one is bound down to the other). The order of our apprehensions and the order of what is apprehended refer now to the very same thing. Besides, even if we adopt this "critical principle," the objection remains that we still could not support the conclusion that *all* succession is rule-determined or caused. For we still have not shown that *a-b* is causally determined if what they are perceptions of are coexisting items. (Yet *a-b* is a *succession* of perceptions, no matter what the perceptions are of, not only if they are of an objective succession.)

It seems there is no plausible way of concluding from the fact 1) that every succession of perceptions *a-b,* which is of α, β, where α-β is successive, is causally determined (in being bound down to the order of α-β), to the fact 2) that every succession (or even every succession of *perceptions*) is causally determined. If we are to make sense of the argument of the Second Analogy, we must give up the idea that claim (ii) is the premise from which the conclusion is taken as directly following.

The problem of the Second Analogy is the possibility of determining appearances as successive. The only function of claim ii above, I suggest, is to *dismiss* the idea that we can determine or relate appearances as successive on the basis of the succession in our perceptions; i.e., we cannot determine α, β as successive on the grounds that our perceptions *a, b* of α, β, respectively, are successive. It is rather the other way around.

> . . . We must derive the *subjective succession* of apprehension from the *objective succession* of appearances. Otherwise the order of apprehension is entirely undetermined and does not distinguish one appearance from another [that is, it does not distinguish a succession α-β from α, β, coexisting]. Since the subjective succession by itself is altogether arbitrary it does not prove anything as to the manner in which the manifold is connected in the object (CPR, A 193 B 238, p. 221).

Kant is claiming that I cannot conclude from the succession of my apprehensions to the succession of what is thus apprehended. Something further is involved, namely that the apprehension is not only successive but irreversible. Bringing in the irreversibility in the apprehension of a succession (as opposed to the reversibility in the apprehension of that which is coexistent) is meant merely to refute the idea that I can determine appearances as successive merely on the basis of my apprehensions. It is not the introduction of a criterion in terms of which we determine a succession as objective. We do not ascertain that what we apprehend is successive by ascertaining that our apprehensions are irreversible.

In this respect, the proof at B 244, A 199–A 256, A 201 (pp. 225–26) is relevant to the argumentation of the other proofs, for in this proof it is emphasized that not only can succession not be determined on the basis of the succession in apprehensions, but that a succession cannot be determined by relating the terms of the succession to absolute (empty) time. Kant says, "Now since absolute time is not an object of perception, this determination of position cannot be derived from the relation of appearances to it. On the contrary the appearances must determine for one another their position in time . . ." (CPR, A 200, B 245, p. 226). Appearances can be determinately related to each other as successive only on the basis of some feature of appearances. According to the present interpretation a succession in the object is a determinate succession, and the determinacy (order) of the succession must be based on features of appearances. All this fits in well with the argument of the First Analogy, where it is claimed that the basis of time-determination (there, the determination of time magnitude) must be found in the objects of perception. All the proofs of the Second Analogy dismiss plausible alternatives to grounding the relation of appearances (in this case as determinately successive) to each other in time on the basis of features of appearances. The proof at B 244–46 rejects the alternative of determining the order of appearances by relating them to absolute (empty) time. The other proofs reject the alternative of determining the order of appearances on the basis of the order of our apprehensions. In section 4.3 we shall see why *causal* determination between appearances is required for determining appearances as successive, if we are to determine this on the basis of features of appearances (or on the basis of what is to be found in the objects of perception).

For the moment let us return to Kant's contention that the order of appearances cannot be determined on the basis of perception. His argument is that the succession in my perceptions does not guarantee a corresponding succession in what my perceptions are of. Now let us note that this claim is not made on the basis of the idea that I might be hallucinating or merely imagining or dreaming; i.e., Kant is saying even if I *actually* perceive α and then *actually* perceive β, I cannot conclude that α actually precedes β.* I may actually perceive a part of a house and then actually perceive another part of a house, and yet the two parts of the house may be actually coexistent. Let us note further that Kant would want to say that in *no* case is perception sufficient to determine the order of what is perceived. For, if in some particular case I could determine that α precedes β, say on the basis of perception alone, then I would not require the concept of causality to determine the succession in this case, and thus causality would not be a *universal* condition of determining succession, and thus not every succession, to be determinable, would have to be causally determined.

Now, given the above two considerations, a difficulty arises. Suppose I perceive at once (nonsuccessively) a ship moving from p to a place further downstream p′ (i.e., I don't perceive "ship at p" and then perceive "ship at p′"; I simply perceive the ship moving from p to p′). Can I not conclude that the state of affairs "ship at p" (α) precedes the state of affairs "ship at p′" (β); i.e., in this case can I not conclude from the fact that I (nonsuccessively) perceive α preceding β, that α does in fact precede β? Remember, we are granting here, as in all cases, that we are actually perceiving and not hallucinating or imagining or dreaming. In other words, if α succeeding β can be made part of the "specious present" of one perception, can we not conclude (granting that we are not concerned with the possibility of hallucination, etc.) that α did succeed β? It seems that in such a case we can determine that α preceded β merely on the basis of perception (without recourse to any causal considerations). Kant, it seems, would deny that a succession could be perceived at once. He says, "The apprehension of the manifold of appearance is always successive" (CPR, A 190, B 235, p. 219). What I wish to indicate is that Kant's argument for the insufficiency in every case of determining succession on the basis of perception alone does seem to rest on this idea that a succession of states is always successively apprehended; a succession is never within the "specious present" of one perception.

The argument of the Second Analogy seeks to show that *all* (not

---

* And thus the point of the Second Analogy is not, as Lovejoy claims, to distinguish dreams and imaginations from real perceptions (see Lovejoy, 1906; in Gram, 1967, pp. 290 ff.).

just most or a great deal of) succession is causally determined. An essential step in this argument is that in *no* case is the order of appearances as successive determinable on the basis of perception alone. This step seems to depend, as we have indicated, on the thesis that apprehension is always successive, in the strong sense that no succession can be apprehended in the specious present of a perception. But to rest the argument of the Second Analogy on this highly problematic thesis seems to be all too precarious. What I want to argue is that there can be found in Kant's statements a justification for the claim that perception is never sufficient for determining time-order, which justification does not depend on the thesis that succession in the object can never be perceived at once (nonsuccessively). This justification is in terms of Kant's conception of time-determination.

11. Kant's Conception of Time-Determination

It must at least be possible for a subject who judges about what is given temporally to determine the position in time of what is given. There are three different kinds of locution by means of which we indicate time location:

> 1) We say that x is happening *now*.
> 2) We say that x happened at 6:02.4 on 4 July 1936; at 6:02.4 on 4 July 1936, 1) and 2) are equivalent.
> 3) We say that x happened before y or after z or at the same time as w.

Locution 1, that x is happening now, can be reduced to 3 according to some such analysis as "x happens at the same time that I utter these words 'x is happening now.' " (This analysis is not circular for 'now' is only mentioned, not used in the definition, and can, if desired, be eliminated altogether.) The word 'now' functions seemingly like a proper name that names a moment of time, but like all proper names it can execute its function only if it is backed up or supported by a reserve of descriptions that, in this case, indicates what (which moment) it is the name of. The descriptions in the case of names for moments of time are in terms of the occupants of time. Thus, *a* is the moment at which a certain event e, say, takes place. In the case of 'now' there is a standard description backing up the name; i.e., the event in terms of which the moment of time named is indicated or specified is the utterance of the sentence that employs the term 'now'.

Similarly, locution 2, that x happens at 6:02.4 on 4 July 1936, depends on locutions of type 3, just in the sense that a dating system is devised in terms of the relative position of events or states of affairs with respect to one another in time. If it made no sense to say that we could determine that the earth is at p before it is at p', then it would make no sense to base a dating system on the revolution of the earth about the sun.

Although locutions of type 3 seem to be the most basic locutions for indicating time position, this third locution, as it stands, does not locate events or states of affairs in time. Determining the order of succession of two states A, B as, say, A-B does determine A's position relative to B. And yet unless we can determine the "place" of the *entire* succession A-B in time, determining the relative position of the terms of the succession vis-à-vis one another is not sufficient for determining the position of either A or B in time. To determine that (B), the acceleration of a car, succeeded (A), the impress of someone's foot upon the gas pedal, is to determine that A occurred before B, but it is not to determine exactly (or approximately) when either A or B occurred, for we have not thus determined at all when the succession A-B as a whole took place.

Now, we can no more determine when the succession A-B took place in relation to absolute time than we can determine that A preceded B by reference to absolute time. To determine when the succession A-B occurred is to determine the position of this succession in relation to still other events $C_1, \ldots C_n$ in time. Suppose that this has been determined to be in the following order C_1-C_2 . . . -C_n —A-B. Again, the question arises *when* this series of events as a whole (and in this order) took place, and again the answer can only be in terms of the relation of this series of events to still other events. Ultimately, the relative position of all events or states of affairs to all other events or states of affairs must be determinable. It is only against the background of this thoroughgoing determinability of any two states or events vis-à-vis one another that the position of any event can be determinable 'in respect of the unity of all time" (CPR, B 219, p. 209). Suppose the relative position of events (or occurrences or states of affairs) A and B is indeterminable. Since the dyadic relation "x's position in time vis-à-vis y is determinable" is a transitive relation, any event whose position is determinable with respect to A would not then have a position determinable with respect to B, and vice versa. We could not then determine C's position, say, "in respect to the unity of all time," but only its position either with respect to the series of events that are determinable vis-à-vis A or the series of events that are determinable vis-à-vis B.

Kant says, "Each alteration in the world is only an extension of an already fixed series" (*Reflexionen Kants,* hereafter RK; p. 303). What I think is meant is that determining the relative position of a succession A-B is irrelevant to determining the position of either A or B in time, unless the position of this succession is itself determinable. This latter requires that the succession A-B be determinable with respect to the position of other events or states of affairs *that collectively form a single series or ordering in which any state of affairs has a fixed position determinable vis-à-vis any other.* The position of any event with respect to this series must be determinable. That the function of causality is linked with the idea not merely of determining that y, say, succeeded x, but with determining the position of an event or state of affairs with respect to *the single series of events* is stated in the following passage. ". . . And though the correlate [the cause] is, indeed, indeterminate it none the less stands in a determining relation to the event as its consequence, *connecting the event in necessary relation with itself in the time-series* [italics mine]" (CPR, A 199, B 244, p. 225).

It is clear from the foregoing that time-determination is a *regulative* matter in the following sense. I determine that B succeeds A. The question arises of what the position is in time of the succession A-B. This position is determined with respect to other states of affairs $C_1, \ldots, C_n$. The question again arises concerning the position of the series of states of affairs A-B-C_1— . . . —C_n in time; i.e., of its position with respect to still other events. I never, so to speak, completely determine the position of B or A in time, since I can only determine their position relative to other events, and these events, in turn, can only be determined as to time-position in terms of still other events. To ask what the position in time of a series of events $C_1, \ldots, C_n$ is, is to ask what its position is relative to other events. (Otherwise we would have to determine its position with respect to absolute [empty] time), and this question (within the context of experience) is always reiterable, under the guiding idea that ultimately *all* events have positions *determinable* in a single series.

Any of the three locutions above indicate the time position of events or states of affairs only against the background of the idea that we *could* go on and determine the position of these events with respect to a context of other events, and that we *could* go on and determine these other events with respect to a still wider context. Suppose we determine that A is after B. Then unless B's position is determinable in time, we have not thus determined A's position. So suppose B is after C and D but before E. Unless C-D-B-E is determinable in time, B's relative position to these other events is useless. But what is it to say that this series is determinable in time, except that it can be related temporally to still other events?

Kant says, "In this third [medium] the essential form of which consists in the synthetic unity of the apperception of all appearances we have found a priori conditions of *complete* and necessary determination of time for all existence in the [field of] appearances, without which even empirical determination of time would be impossible [italics mine]" (CPR, A 217, B 264, p. 238). We can determine that A precedes B. That A precedes B is an empirical matter (it cannot be known a priori). This *empirical determination* is only possible (as a determination of the position of either A or B in time) against the background of a *complete* determinability of the position of all events in time vis-à-vis one another; complete determinability is not in itself an empirical matter.

To return to our original problem (to show that perception is, in all cases, insufficient for determining time-position), even if the succession of B upon A can be made part of the specious present of a perception (i.e., even if it can be perceived nonsuccessively), this does not mean that either B's or A's determinate position in time is thereby perceived. All that is perceived is that B follows A. When B follows A (i.e., what the position of the succession as a whole is) is not thereby perceived or determined. The same point holds in the case of perceiving two simultaneous events or states of affairs C, D. That C and D happen (or obtain) at the same time is not sufficient for determining the position of either C or D in time, for it is not thereby determined when the simultaneous occurrence happened (i.e., when it happened in relation to other events). In other words, the fact that I can perceive x preceding y or x and y happening at the same time shows merely that I can perceive time relations of appearances; it does not show that I can thereby perceive the time position of the relata (which is something more than the position of the perceived relata vis-à-vis merely one another).

12. The Argument of the Second Analogy

If time-position cannot be determined by perception or by reference to empty time, then the determinability of the temporal order of events (or states) must be in terms of (based on) some feature (or features) of appearances, in terms of some feature to be found in the objects of perception. There are no monadic predicates P1 and P2 such that x being P1 and Y being P2 implies anything about the order of x and y, unless, perhaps, there is some rule connecting the instantiation of P1 in x with the instantiation of P2 in y. For example, let P1 be the mass m1 of a piece of radium x and P2 be the mass of m2 of that piece of radium at some other time. That m1 is, say, less than m2 implies nothing definite about the relative order of x being P1 and x being P2 except in terms of a rule to the effect that radium (in certain circumstances) undergoes radioactive decay (as opposed to say, radioactive augumentation). There is nothing about appearances (no feature of appearances) taken by themselves that determines appearances to have a certain order vis-à-vis one another, except in terms of some rule that orders the appearances on the basis of these features.

What is required is some way of connecting two events or states x and y on the basis of characteristics of appearances (on the basis of what kind of events x and y are either qualitatively and/or quantitatively). In other words, we need something like the following: if *a* is P1 (event x or state x) and *b* is P1 (event y or state y), then *a* is prior to *b* (or *a* being p1 is prior to *b* being P_2). Further, if we are to connect x and y as noncoexistent (as successive), the rule relating x and y to each other on the basis of features of appearances must be an asymmetrical one. By this I do not mean that if *a* being P1 and *b* being P2 is sufficient, in a particular case, for concluding that *a* being P1 is prior to *b* being P2, then the predicates P1 and P2 are such that if any *a'* is P1 and any *b'* is P2, then *a'* being P1 is prior to *b'* being P2. The situation in which *a* is P1 and *b* is P2 may be relevantly different from the situation in which *a'* is P1 and *b'* is P2. Thus, for example, if an auto at time t1 is rust-free (P1) and at time t2 is corroded (P2), any conclusion as to the temporal order of these two states (whether t1 precedes or succeeds t2) depends on the circumstances (on whether, e.g., the auto has ever been repainted, etc.). We do not require assymetrical rules in the sense that we need features P1 and P2 such that anything that is P1 is precedent to that thing's being P2. What we require are features P1 and P2 that, in certain circumstances, allow us to conclude that something being P1 is prior to it being P2, although in other circumstances we may conclude that something being P1 is posterior to it being P2. What is required is that, in the particular circumstances, we can conclude on the basis of features of appearances to some asymmetrical temporal ordering between events or states of affairs.

I do not think it would be far wrong to define a causal law, in the most general (and skeletal) sense, as a rule that enables us to order events temporally as asymmetric on the basis of features of the events (taking into consideration features of the circumstances). Of course we usually think of other aspects involved in causal laws, most notably perhaps universality and necessity of connection. We shall argue in section 18 that if a causal law is to serve as a rule for ordering events temporally on the basis of what kind of events they are (and the circumstances of their occurrence), then causal laws must be universal and necessary in a certain sense. For the moment, however, we can outline Kant's argument as follows:

1) The determinability of the order of events as non-coexistent must be grounded on features of appearances.

2) The determinability of the order of events requires that we be able to infer from features of appearances the relative order of the events.

3) Thus, we must have rules that enable us to conclude, on the basis of features of appearances, that events are ordered in a certain way (rules that enable us to make the transition from real features of appearances to temporal order).

4) But a rule that enables us to conclude that events are ordered in a certain way asymmetrically (as non-coexistent) on the basis of features of appearances (features of the events and of the surrounding circumstances) is (ipso facto, according to the skeletal definition) a causal law.

5) Therefore, causal laws are required for the determinability of the order of appearances as successive.

Once we have eliminated reference to absolute time and mere perception as ways of determining the time-order of events or states of affairs, and thus realize that this determination must proceed on the basis of what is to be found in the objects of perception, then the transition to causality as a condition of time-determination proceeds, for Kant, straightforwardly. We require a means of concluding from features of events or states of affairs to their temporal ordering; i.e., we require rules that license inferences ("inference tickets" in Ryle's terminology) from features of events or states of affairs to temporal ordering. But the notion of a rule that licenses such inferences is precisely the core of the notion of a causal law. The transition from (i) time-determination must be based on features of appearances, to (ii) time-determination requires causal laws, is, for Kant, an obvious transition, *for a causal law is precisely a rule that allows us, on the basis of features of appearances, to conclude to a certain temporal ordering of appearances.* The very schema of causality indicates why Kant should take this transition to be obvious. "It consists therefore in the succession of the manifold, insofar as that succession is subject to a rule [and thus determinable on the basis of features of the terms of the succession]." He also says, "Thus, the relation of appearances (as possible perceptions) according to which the subsequent event, that which happens, is as to its existence, determined in time by something preceding, in conformity with a rule—*in other words,* the relation of cause and effect —is the condition . . . [italics mine]" (CPR, A 202, B 247, p. 227; see also B 163, p. 172).

Kant's conclusion in the second Analogy has often been thought to be an exaggeration of the more plausible claim that experience would be impossible unless there were a certain amount of regularity and order among objects. This regularity or order however, it is claimed, need not be thoroughgoing or complete, as Kant, supposedly, thinks it must. Thus, Strawson says,

> Tentatively, then, we may suppose that while perceptions of the world may reveal *some* objective changes which we can characterize as inexplicable, quite unpredictable or utterly random, they can do so only against a background of persistences and alterations which we recognize as explicable, predictable, and regular. . . . We could accommodate some inexplicable objective change, and some mere exceptions to our law-like expectations, without damage to the necessary but loosely woven mesh of

our concepts of the objective (Strawson, 1966, pp. 144–46).

G. J. Warnock, discussing Kant's argument, says,

> It is true that if there were *too many* random, inexplicable, quite unforeseeable happenings, we should find ourselves not merely in practical but also in linguistic difficulties. . . . What this shows, however, is that we could not speak and act as we do if there were *too much* disorder and chaos in our environment; it does not show that we could not tolerate any at all (Warnock; in Flew, 1961).

Now this sort of objection to Kant assumes that in the Second Analogy Kant is arguing that there must be complete *regularity* and *order* in our experience. In the Second Analogy Kant is arguing that all events must be governed by causal laws, not that our experience must be so totally ordered that we can discover in all (or even in many) cases what these causal laws are. Paton gets this point right. He says,

> So far as I can see, such assumptions are not a consequence of the principle of causality, nor have they been justified by any argument. It is theoretically possible that in a universe governed throughout by causal laws there might be no repetitions [which would enable us to discover what these laws are] (Paton, 1936, 2:276).

As we have seen in section 11, we determine the time position of a specific event x in terms of when x occurred relative to other events, under the assumption that we could go on and determine its position relative to all other events. But this latter is merely a regulative idea; i.e., we do not actually determine x's position vis-à-vis all other events. All that we require is that this position be determinable. Thus, we determine x as having a certain position in a series of events $C_1, C_2 \ldots x \ldots, C_n, C_{n+1}$. This is to determine x's position in time only under the assumption that we could go on and determine the place of this series in time; i.e., its position vis-à-vis still other events. What is required is the assumption that the position of any event be determinable with respect to any other event. This, by the argument of the Second Analogy, requires that any two events be causally connected. This is not to say that given any pair of events, x, y, one will be the cause of the other, but rather that given any two events x, y, we can trace the connection between them in terms of causal rules.

It is this determinability of *all* events or states of affairs in time that requires thoroughgoing causal connection among all events. This determinability of all events in time is a regulative idea, under which assumption determining the time position of specific events vis-à-vis one another takes place. It is precisely because this is a regulative idea that we do not require that our experience be so completely orderly that we can actually trace the connection between any two events in terms of specific causal laws.

Kant is not arguing in the Second Analogy that we must actually determine the relative position of any two events in time. This would indeed require that we have at our disposal a complete system of particular causal laws that we know to obtain of what is given through experience. He is arguing rather that the relative position of any two events in time must be determinable; *if* we knew the actual causal connections, we could actually determine the position of any event vis-à-vis every other event. This latter makes no claim at all concerning the stock (or range) of particular (specific) causal laws at our disposal, and thus no claim at all concerning how much regularity and order must be actually exhibited to us in our experience. The thoroughgoing connection according to causal laws is required for the thoroughgoing determinability of all events vis-à-vis all other events in time. Thoroughgoing order or regularity would be required for the thoroughgoing actual determination of all events vis-à-vis all other events in time. But Kant is not arguing that this latter is what is presupposed in determining the position of specific events in time; it is only the former that is required.

It is, after all, in the "Appendix to the Transcendental Dialectic" (not in the Second Analogy) that Kant discusses the question of order or regularity. He there states quite explicitly that we cannot determine a priori how much order our experience shall exhibit, nor how much order it must exhibit if experience (involving judgment) is to be possible. He says,

> And in accordance with this latter principle, homogeneity is necessarily presupposed in the manifold of possible experience (although we are not in a position to deter-

mine in *a priori* fashion its degree); for in the absence of homogeneity, no empirical concepts, and therefore no experience, would be possible (CPR, A 654, B 682, pp. 539–40).

13. The Third Analogy

The argument of the Third Analogy is from the determinability of appearances as coexisting in and through time to dynamical community or interaction as the condition of such determinability. The structure of the argument closely parallels that of the Second Analogy. Kant begins by saying, "Things are coexistent when in empirical intuition the perceptions of them can follow upon one another reciprocally" (CPR, B 257, p. 233). As we have seen, this fact distinguishes the successive perception of what is coexistent from the successive perception of what is successive. We do not determine that A and B are coexistent by determining that our perceptions of A and B are reversible. I perceive A and then perceive B. If A and B coexist through the time of my successive perceptions, then it was possible to have perceived B and then have perceived A and, in so doing, to have perceived the same state of affairs (the coexistence of A and B through time), but I do not ascertain that A and B coexist by ascertaining that my perceptions might have been in the reverse order. Again, we derive facts about the subjective order of our perceptions (i.e., whether the order is reversible) from the objective temporal connection of the appearances that are perceived (whether they coexist). Kant says,

> The synthesis of imagination in apprehension would only reveal that the one perception is in the subject when the other is not there, and vice-versa, but not that the objects are coexistent, that is, that if the one exists, the other exists at the same time, *and that it is only because they thus coexist* that the perceptions are able to follow one another reciprocally [italics mine] (CPR, B 257, pp. 233–34).

Thus, the knowledge of appearances as coexisting is not grounded on the knowledge of the reversibility in the order of our perceptions. Rather, the reversibility in the order of our perceptions is based on the fact that they are perceptions of appearances that coexist through the time of the perceptions.

Again, Kant denies that we can ascertain that appearances coexist by relating them to (absolute) empty time. The ground of our knowledge of the coexistence of appearances through time must be found in the appearances themselves (in the objects of perception). In other words, what is required are rules that enable us, based on features of appearances, to conclude to the coexistence of items; a rule such as, if x is P1 and y is P2, then x being P1 is coexistent with (exists at or through the same time as) y being P2 (depending, of course, on the circumstances). To say there is a rule determining the coexistence of x and y on the basis of features of x and y is (skeletally) to say that x and y are in (direct or indirect) mutual or reciprocal interaction. (Just as a causal rule is a rule enabling us to infer from features of appearances that they are ordered in a determinate way as successive, so a law of interaction is a rule enabling us to infer from features of appearances that they are simultaneous and/or coexistent.) "The schema of community or reciprocity, the reciprocal causality of substances in respect of their accidents, *is the coexistence, according to a universal rule,* of the determinations of the one substance with those of the other [italics mine]" (CPR, A 144, B 184, p. 185).

In general terms, then, the argument of the Second and Third Analogies proceeds as follows:

> 1) Determining the position of an event or state of affairs in time is always determining its position relative to other events or states of affairs, and always on the presupposition that the position of the event could be determined relatively to all other events.
>
> 2) This thoroughgoing determinability is not possible by means of perception or by relating events individually to absolute time, or time by itself.
>
> 3) Thus, this determinability must be based on features of the objects of perception.
>
> 4) No features of objects of perception (states of affairs or events) allow us to infer their relative temporal order except in terms of rules that license such inferences. Thus, if x is P and y is P′, this, in itself, tells us nothing

about the relative temporal order of x and y unless there is some rule that determines this order on the basis of the fact that x and y are P and P′ (in certain circumstances), respectively.

5) Thus the determinability of the relative order of events (according to the dimension—before, after, at the same time) is only possible through rules that license inferences from features of events to their temporal order. The thoroughgoing determinability of the relative order of all events requires the thoroughgoing connection of events according to such rules.

6) But a rule that allows us to infer, on the basis of certain features of events or states of affairs, that these events or states of affairs are temporally ordered in a certain way is simply the core notion of

a) a causal law, if the inferred temporal ordering is that the events or states are successive;

b) a law of interaction or community, if the temporal ordering inferred is that the states are simultaneous or coexist through time.

7) We may add the result of the First Analogy, that a) the magnitude of a time interval between events is only determinable in terms of the action of some substance that persists through that interval, and b) it is only states of substance that can be proper relata for succession and simultaneity.

The weakest step in the argument is step 6. As we shall see in sections 14 and 15, causal laws cannot be distinguished from laws of interaction or dynamical community according to the principle that the former are rules for determining the time-order of appearances as successive, while the latter are rules for determining the time-order of appearances as simultaneous or coexistent through time. In this respect, the separation of the argument into two sections, the Second Analogy and the Third Analogy, is artificial and forced. There is a generic sense of causal law in which Newton's law of gravitation, say (the paradigm of a law of interaction), is a causal law. This generic sense of causal law is the same as the notion of a real connection of objects according to rules. We may replace 6 by the following:

6′) But a rule that allows us to infer on the basis of certain features of events or states of affairs that these events or states of affairs are temporally ordered in a certain way is just the core idea of a causal law (where causal law is used in the generic sense in which it is synonymous with rule-governed real connection).* With 6′ replacing 6, the argument is immune to the difficulties we shall discuss in Sections 14 and 15, and yet it essentially accomplishes Kant's purpose of showing that experience is possible only through a real connection of objects of experience. In other words, the difficulties in step 6, which we shall discuss in sections 14 and 15, ought to be regarded as difficulties in detail, not as difficulties that destroy the general cogency of the argument.

In section 16 we discuss the notion of an "accidental" occurrence, and in section 17, the notion of teleological causality. In section 18 we discuss in what sense a causal connection involves necessity and universality. Section 18 cannot be regarded as dealing merely with a detail of the argument, for it is a central aspect of Kant's notion of a causal connection that it be a necessary and universal connection. It is the necessity and universality of the connection that makes the concept of causality an a priori one. Further, the kind of necessity and universality involved is intimately linked to the idea that only a subject who judges under the nonmaterial hypothetical form can employ the concept of causality, and thus to the idea that causality is an epistemic concept (see p. 51, above). In other words, what we have to show in section 18 is that the argument of the Analogies proves that the *full-fledged* notion of causality (as an epistemic notion, and as a concept involving necessity and universality) must be employed if time-determination (and thus ultimately judging about what is given in experience) is to be possible.

14. *Simultaneity of Cause and Effect*

At A 203, B 248, Kant says, "But in the moment in which the effect first comes to be, it is invariably simultaneous with the causality of

---

* See CPR, A 145 B 184, p. 185, where Kant says, "The schema of relation [in general] is the connecting of perceptions with one another at all times according to a rule of time-determination."

its cause." If cause and effect are simultaneous, then how can causality (the schema of causality) serve to determine appearances as non-successive? Kant's explanation is that "it is the *order* of time, not the lapse of time with which we have to reckon." Now it is true that causality (as far as the Second Analogy is concerned) is employed to determine time-order. The lapse of time is discussed in the First Analogy. As we have seen, causality is also involved in determining time-lapse, in the sense that it is the action of a substance that serves as the substratum of the determination of time intervals, and the "regularity" of the action is a function of causal conditions (see p. 69, above). That the Second Analogy is concerned with time-*order* does not obviate the apparent difficulty of the cause being simultaneous with the effect, for if the cause is simultaneous with the effect then the time-order of the cause and effect is that they are simultaneous. How can we determine that x precedes y on the basis of causality if the cause is simultaneous (Kant says, invariably so) with the effect? Kant says, "The time between the causality of the cause and its immediate effect may be a *vanishing* quantity, and they may thus be simultaneous; but the relation of the one to the other will always still remain determinable in time." Certainly the relation of the one to the other will be determinable, but it seems that the cause and effect will be determinable as simultaneous, although simultaneity is supposed to be determined by interaction, not causality. Kant goes on to explain how to distinguish cause and effect when they are simultaneous. He says, "I still distinguish the two through the time relation of their dynamical connections. For if I lay the ball on the cushion a hollow follows upon the previous flat smooth shape; but if (for any reason) there previously exists a hollow in the cushion, a leaden ball does not follow upon it." Let us note that we are here offered an analysis of how to distinguish cause and effect when they are simultaneous. But this seems perfectly irrelevant if we take the problem to be, not how to distinguish cause and effect but, having determined what caused what, how we can infer some succession in appearances. Kant seems to be saying that the effect could have happened without the cause, but that the cause could not have happened without the effect. This may be true, but the problem remains: how are we to conclude from this fact to any succession in the appearances when the cause and the effect simultaneously occur?

The answer to this problem depends on an understanding of the distinction between a causal rule and the condition of applying that rule (in particular, the condition that can be singled out as the cause). Let us take as an example the leaden ball and the hollowing of the cushion. What I suggest is that the succession to be determined in this case is not a) the hollowing of the cushion upon b) the laying upon the cushion of a leaden ball. These are simultaneous. *Rather, the succession is in the two states of the cushion.* First, (i) the cushion is flat, then (ii) the cushion is hollowed out. Let us note that (i) and (ii) could not (logically) be simultaneous. No matter how little time it took for the cushion to change from one state to the other, even if it tends to vanish, the two states cannot be simultaneous. One thing cannot be in two conflicting states at the same time. "If a substance passes from one state *a*, to another *b*, the point of time of the second is distinct from that of the first, and follows upon it" (CPR, A 207, B 253, p. 230). Now the causal rule connecting (i) and (ii) would be something like the following. L_1: If a force of m lbs. is exerted on a cushion of such and such resiliency, mass, and so on, then the cushion will depress to such and such a hollowed out shape. L_1 asserts a temporal succession of states of the cushion, given that a certain force is exerted. Thus, L_1 conforms to the schema of causality as asserting a temporal succession. The conditions of applying L_1 include determining the resiliency and mass of the cushion and the amount of force exerted on the cushion. Among the conditions, the exertion of a force can be singled out as *the* condition (the initiating condition or the cause) because all of the other conditions are, in a sense, "standing" conditions. Although the exact depression of the cushion depends as much on its resiliency as on the amount of force exerted, there is still a sense in which the exertion of a force ought to be singled out as the cause. The exact way in which the cushion undergoes a change of state, how much, e.g., it will hollow out, depends as much on its resiliency as on the amount of force exerted; but the exertion of some force accounts for there being any change of state at all, in a way that the resiliency does not. Thus, we can pick out the exertion of force as *the* condition of applying L_1.

In our particular example, the laying of the leaden ball upon the cushion is the condition of applying the causal rule L_1. (L_1 as we have formulated it is, perhaps, too highly specified. A dynamical rule would not usually characterize what undergoes the change of state as a cushion, and the condition of applying L_1 would not be characterized as a leaden ball, but rather as a body with a certain mass, although this is irrelevant to our point.) That this condition is simultaneous with the change of state of the cushion (the force acts through the whole change of state) does not detract from the fact that the *rule* applied on the basis of this condition asserts a *succession* of states in the cushion. *In other words, a causal rule may assert a succession of states whether or not the condition of applying the rule singled out as the cause of the succession precedes or is simultaneous with the effect (the effect being a succession of states.)*

L$_1$ does not assert a succession between the cause (the action of the leaden ball) and the effect (the succession of states of the cushion). More generally, the causal rule does not assert that the cause precedes the effect; what it asserts is the "order" and "character" of the change, or of the succession of states, which constitutes the effect. (See p. 230, n. *a,* where Kant says that an effect is always a change of state or a succession of states.) It asserts this order and character of the succession on the basis of a condition, irrespective of whether or not the condition singled out as the cause is precedent to the effect (the succession) or simultaneous with it.

Kant says, "Therefore, since there certainly is something that follows (i.e., that is *apprehended* as following), I must refer it necessarily to something else which precedes it and upon which it follows in conformity with a rule, that is, of necessity" (CPR, A 194, B 239, p. 222). Now what follows from the cause (the effect) is a succession of states (an effect is always a change, a succession of states of affairs). In saying that the effect follows in conformity with a rule, we are not saying that the effect follows after the cause z but rather that the effect (the succession of states in a particular order and with a particular character) follows from the cause z, in the sense that we connect the two states (the succession of which constitutes the effect) according to a rule, where z is the condition of applying this rule. In other words, the succession is the succession of states constituting the effect, not the succession between the cause and the effect. It is determined by the cause in the sense that the cause serves as the condition for applying the rule, where the rule asserts the succession of states is ordered in a certain way, given that certain conditions (one of which is singled out as the cause) obtain.

Kant says, "The objective succession will therefore consist in that order according to which, *in conformity with a rule,* the apprehension of that which happens follows upon the apprehension of that which precedes" (CPR, A 194, B 238, p. 222). Now the objective succession is not a succession of an effect after a cause, but a succession of states of affairs constituting the effect. The order of this succession must proceed (can only be determined) in conformity with a rule. Kant proceeds, "In conformity with such a rule there must lie in that which precedes an event *the condition of a rule* according to which this event invariably and necessarily follows" [italics mine]" (CPR, A 194, B 239, p. 222). Now the succession of states does not follow after the cause; it follows from the cause in conformity with a rule. Schematically, the rule states that if z obtains, then x precedes y. Thus, given z, the succession of y upon x follows(logically) from the rule (or, given the rule, the effect follows from the cause). Kant is wrong to say that the condition of applying the rule "must lie in that which precedes an event"; i.e., in what comes before the succession of states that constitutes the event. His example of the leaden ball and the cushion shows that the condition (the force exerted by the leaden ball) may (perhaps must) be simultaneous with the succession of states of affairs that constitutes the effect. What is true is that the rule connecting the states of affairs (the succession of which constitutes the effect) asserts that the states of affairs are ordered successively in a determinate manner. The rule asserts a succession (in this sense) whether or not the condition of applying the rule is to be found in what precedes the succession, or in what is simultaneous with the succession.

It is only if we take the function of causality to be 1) determining that event z precedes event z', since z is the cause of z', rather than 2) determining that the state of affairs x precedes the state of affairs y (where x-y constitutes the effect z'), since L_1 asserts or implies that x precedes y on the condition that z obtains; it is only if we confuse 2 with 1, I am saying, that the fact that causes may be simultaneous with their effects conflicts with the function of causal laws, viz., the determinability of appearances as successive.

Wolff says,

> ... for Kant really is dealing with two distinct concepts of causation. The first is that of necessary succession, deriving from the analysis of Hume. ... The second is the scientific concept of functional interdependence, expressed in such equations as the laws of motion. ... It is not clear how Kant can relate these two concepts to one another ... (1963, p. 292).

Wolff thinks the first concept of causation is dealt with in the Second Analogy while the second concept is (or ought to have been) dealt with in the Third Analogy. Now the distinction between a causal rule and the condition of applying that rule provides, I suggest, the way to relate what Wolff thinks are two different concepts of causation. Thus, in the example of the cushion, the impress of the cushion is functionally dependent on the amount of force exerted (among other things). By that I mean the "amount" or "degree" or "speed" of impress is calculable from the force in terms of dynamical laws. This is perfectly compatible with saying that the succession of states in the cushion is a necessary succession given the impress of force. Wolff is correct to point out that "The law F = ma, for example, does not state that something B, invariably follows something else A" (1963, p. 292), but he is wrong to conclude that this fact divorces the notion of causality from that of necessary succession or succession in accordance with a rule. For the law F = ma, applied in specific instances, certainly implies that an acceleration (which is a succession of states or a change of state) is, given the conditions of applying the law, a necessary succession. Although the law itself may not assert a succession of states, still successions of states take place in conformity with this law.

15. *Causation and Interaction*

The simultaneity of cause and effect brings up the problem of how to distinguish a causal connection and reciprocal interaction. As we have indicated, in one sense the idea of a causal connection (a connection according to causal laws) is a generic idea that includes mutual interaction as one specific example of such connection. Newton's law of gravitational attraction is certainly a causal law in the sense that it is an explanation of certain phenomena according to principles, yet bodies conforming to this law provide perhaps the paradigm illustration of things in mutual interaction. In the sense that causal laws are considered generically as explanations of phenomena, bodies in mutual interaction act in accordance with causal laws. Yet Kant wishes to distinguish causal connection from mutual interaction; i.e., he wishes to distinguish cases in which one would say that x is the cause of y from cases where x and y are in mutual interaction. If we accept the idea that causes can (and perhaps must) be simultaneous with their effects, then it will not do to say that x is the cause of y only if x is temporally prior to y, whereas x and y are in mutual interaction only if neither is temporally prior to the other.

I do not intend to give a general and comprehensive analysis of the distinction between causation and mutual interaction. The only importance, for our purposes, of investigating this distinction is that Kant seems to think that causation is peculiarly involved in determining succession, whereas interaction is peculiarly involved in determining simultaneity or coexistence. I shall discuss in detail certain specific cases that will show clearly enough that, on any plausible construal of the distinction between causation and interaction, determining succession cannot be correlated specifically with causation, and similarly determining simultaneity or coexistence cannot be correlated specifically with mutual interaction.

Suppose we have two billiard balls, *b* and *c*, at rest, and they are hit by a moving billiard ball *a*, whereupon *b* and *c* move off in different directions (Fig. 3).

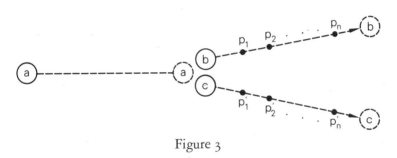

Figure 3

We thus have two series of successive states: 1) *b* at place p1, *b* at p2, ..., *b* at pn; 2) *c* at p1', *c* at p2', ..., *c* at pn'. Again, we have a dynamical law L_1 that describes the motion of *b* and *c* as a function of various factors—the elasticity of the billiard balls, the direction of the acting force (the angle at which *a* hit *b*, and the angle at which *a* hit *c*), the magnitude of the acting force (the momentum of *a*), the coefficient of friction of *b* and *c* with respect to the billiard table, and so on. Once again, the impact of *a* (the impact of a body having a certain momentum) may be singled out as *the* condition (the initiating condition) that allows us to apply the law L_1. The question arises whether the impact of a with b and c (which is picked out as the initiating condition) is a case of causation or mutual interaction. In other words, is the motion of b and c due to an interaction with a or is it caused by the impact of a? One obvious answer, it seems, is both, for its being due to the interaction of b and c with a and its being caused by the impact of a are not mutually exclusive characterizations (especially since for Kant, following Newton, one body acting upon another is always acted upon by that other body).

What I want to suggest is that whether we take the motion of b and c to be the result of their interaction with a or to be the result (the effect) of a hitting b and c (the causal *action* of a upon b and c) depends in this case on whether we relate the motion of b and c to the motion of a after the collision of a with b and c.

Case 1: Suppose first that we are interested in determining b's position with respect to c (but not their positions with respect to a). Let us first note that L_1 can serve *both* as a rule for simultaneity and a rule for succession. On the basis of L_1 and the various factors that enable us to calculate in accordance with L_1, we can determine that c must be at p_1' when b is at p_1; i.e., that the two states, "b at p_1," "c at p_1'," are simultaneous. Now the position of b at any time is not directly a function of the position of c or vice versa; i.e., b and c are not in any important sense in mutual interaction. (Of course there may be gravitational attraction between b and c, but this attraction can certainly be disregarded.) Although b's position at any moment is not a function of c's position at any moment, still b's position at any moment is connected to c's position at any moment according to a rule, namely L_1; b would not be at p_i unless c were at p_i' at that time, and vice versa (given, of course, the conditions of applying L_1 in this case).

Now suppose we calculate, as surely we can, that b must have been at p_1 before c was at p_2'. In other words, we can employ L_1 to determine a succession of states as well as a simultaneous occurrence of states. As we have seen (in section 14), employing L_1 as a rule for determining succession does not imply that these two states are related as cause and effect (which in the present case they are not; b being at p_1 is certainly not the cause of c being at p_2'). Thus, determining "b at p_1," "c at p_2" as successive does not depend on b at p_1 being the cause of c at p_2', and determining "b at p_1," "c at p_1'" as simultaneous does not depend on these two states being states of mutually interacting substances (b and c are not in any important sense in mutual interaction). Further, the same law applied on the basis of the same conditions can be used to determine both succession and coexistence of states.

We have successive states "b at p1," "c at p2'," and simultaneous states "b at p1," "c at p1'." If we ask how the succession of states, or equally how the simultaneity of states, is related to the impact of a, we would not say, e.g., that b at p1 is prior to c at p2' because of the interaction of b and c with a. Rather, we would say that the impact of a *caused* the succession of states "b at p1," "c at p2'," even though we may grant that a, in acting upon b and c, was in turn acted upon by both b and c. The reason for this is that the action of b and c upon a is irrelevant to the relative positions of b and c, which is what we are concerned to determine. The result of the action of b and c upon a is a certain change in direction and speed of the motion of a after the collision. But in determining the position of b and c with respect to one another, we are not comparing either of their positions with respect to a, and thus we can leave out all consideration of what happened to a after (and as a result of) the collision. In other words, we do not have to take into account if or how either b or c acted upon a.

We can summarize the points of Case 1 as follows:

> 1) We can use the same law (L_1) under the same conditions (the collision) to determine both succession and simultaneity of states.
>
> 2) We can say the succession of states (b at p1, c at p2') was caused by the impact of a, rather than that it was the result of an interaction of a with b and c, because the action of b and c upon a is irrelevant to determining this particular succession, We say the very same thing about the existence of two states b at p1, c at p1' at the same time. In other words, point 1 above can be strengthened to say, we can use the same law (L_1) under the same *description* of the initiating condition (as a case of causation rather than interaction) to determine both succession and simultaneity).

Case 2: Suppose now that we wish to determine the relative position of b and c with respect to a after the collision:

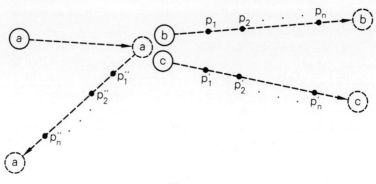

Figure 4

Again, in terms of L_1 and certain conditions of application we can determine (calculate), for example, that 1) a at $p1''$, b at $p1$ are simultaneous states; 2) a at $p1''$, b at $p2$ are successive. In other words, from L_1 and certain conditions of application, a must be at $p1''$ when b is at $p1$, and a must be at $p1''$ before b is at $p2$. The coexistence of a at $p1''$ with b at $p1$, and the succession of b at $p2$ after a at $p1''$ follows (logically) from L_1 and the conditions of applying L_1. Now in Case 2 we would say that the simultaneous occurrence of a at $p1''$ and b at $p1$ is a result of the interaction between a and b, for we now must take into account not only the fact that a hit b, but also that b, in being hit by a, in turn acted upon a. We would say the very same thing for the very same reason about the succession of states a at $p1''$, b at $p2$; i.e., that the succession is the result of an interaction between a and b.

Now notice that in both Case 1 and Case 2 we are applying the same law under the same conditions in order to determine both succession and simultaneity of states. In both cases we single out the collision of a with b and c as "the" condition of applying the law. In Case 1 the succession or coexistence of states determined in accordance with the law is said to be due to the action of a upon b and c. In Case 2, the succession or coexistence of states determined in accordance with the law is said to be due to the interaction of a and b (and, of course, in a perfectly analogous manner, if we were determining the position of c with respect to a, a succession or coexistence of states would be said to be due to the interaction of a and c). In both cases the same condition is picked out as the initiating condition, but in Case 1 it is described as the action of one thing upon another, whereas in Case 2 it is described as the interaction of two things. The way we describe the initiating condition is completely independent of whether, in accordance with the law, we are determining succession or coexistence of states. (We can apply the same sort of reasoning to the example of the leaden ball and the cushion. In determining the succession of states of the cushion in accordance with a dynamical law, the succession is said to be due to the action of the leaden ball [the impress of force], not to the interaction of the ball with the cushion, for in assessing the succession of states in the cushion the [re]action of the cushion upon the ball is irrelevant. If, on the other hand, we are determining the changes of state in the motion of the leaden ball [i.e., its retardation until it comes to rest on the depressed cushion], this change of state would be due to the resistance of the cushion; i.e., to the action of the cushion upon the ball. Here, the action of the ball upon the cushion is not considered because the result of this action [the change of state in the cushion] is not what is being considered.)

Let us turn now to a different example. In the example just discussed, both in Case 1 and Case 2 there was one condition that could be sensibly singled out as "the" condition of applying the law in terms of which the succession or coexistence of states was to be determined, namely, the collision of a with b and c. We now discuss an example in which this is not the case. The example I have in mind is the one Kant gives in the Third Analogy, namely, the interaction of the earth and the moon. The position of the earth and the moon is a function of their interaction with each other and their interaction with other bodies of the solar system. Depending on certain conditions such as the masses of the various bodies, their distance from one another, and so on, we can determine in accordance with the law of gravitational attraction (L_2) that the earth being at a certain place p_1 is simultaneous with the moon being at p_2. This simultaneity of states of affairs is thus determined in accordance with a rule (the law of gravity). Now none of the conditions of applying this law can be singled out as "the" condition of application, in the sense in which the impact of a could be singled out in our previous example. Nevertheless, we would say that the simultaneity of states "earth at p_1, moon at p_2" is due to the interaction of the bodies of the solar system. Notice once again that, in terms of the same law (L_2) applied under the same conditions, we can determine succession of states as well as simultaneity of states. For example, we can determine that the earth being at p1 is prior to the moon being at p3. Similarly, this succession of states can be said to be due to the interaction of the bodies of the solar system.

Now suppose we wished to determine the sequence of states "moon at p2, moon at p3." We can do this again in terms of the law of gravitational attraction and certain conditions of applying this law (masses of solar bodies, distance between solar bodies, etc.). In other words, "moon at p2, moon at p3" is a succession of states according to a rule. Prima facie (and in analogy with our other example), one might think to say that this succession of states is not due to the interaction of the moon with other bodies, but rather that it is due to the *action* of other bodies upon the moon, for the reason that we are not interested in determining the position of any other bodies besides the moon, and thus the effect that the moon has upon these other bodies can be disregarded. This line of reasoning, though appropriate enough in our previous examples, is not appropriate in this case for the reason that here the result of the action of the moon upon other bodies cannot be disregarded in determining what the action of other bodies upon the moon shall be. That the moon will be at p3 at a certain time t is due, in part, to the position of the earth prior to t, but the position of the earth prior to t is dependent upon the position of the moon (at p2, say) prior to t. In Case 1 of our previous example the effect of *a* on the motion of *b* and *c* did not depend on what happened to *a* after the impact, and thus the motion of *a* after the impact (and hence the action of *b* and *c* upon *a* that produced this motion) could be disregarded. In the present example, the action of the moon upon the earth cannot be disregarded, and thus the succession of states moon at p2, moon at p3 is said to be due to the *interaction* of the moon with other solar bodies.

One difference between the present example and Case 2 of the previous example (where a succession *b* at p2, *a* at p1″ was also said to be due to an interaction of *a* and *b*) is that in this example the interaction between the moon and the earth need not be traced back to an event that initiated the interaction. By this I do not mean to imply that the solar system as presently constituted (and as presently interacting) had no beginning, only that whether and how it began is irrelevant to our considering the moon and earth as being in interaction. In Case 2 of the previous example, the collision of *a* and *b* constitutes the interaction between *a* and *b*. After *a* and *b* collide, they do not continue to interact; they merely "play out," so to speak, the effect of the initial interaction, viz., the collision or the impact. One way of seeing this is to notice that the relative motion of b and c only makes sense in terms of the collision, whereas the relative motion of the earth and moon makes sense without regard to any initiating cause.

We need not go into whether Kant would consider Case 2 of the previous example to be a genuine case of interaction. He certainly would consider the moon and the earth to be in interaction. From this latter example it seems clear enough that interaction as well as causal connection can be used to determine succession (the succession of states of the moon at different locations is due to the interaction of the moon with other solar bodies). From Case 1 of the previous example, it seems clear that causality as well as interaction can be used to determine simultaneity or coexistence of states. The simultaneity of b being at p1 with c being at p1' is due to the causal action of a upon b and c, not to any interaction between b and c, or any interaction of b and c with a. Thus, we cannot accept the claim that the schema of causality is *succession* according to a rule, whereas the schema of mutual interaction or community is simultaneity or coexistence according to a rule. The succession of the states of the moon (it being at a series of different locations) is in accordance with a rule, but it is due to an interaction of the moon with other bodies. On the other hand (Case 1), b being at p1 and c being at p1' is a coexistence of states according to a rule, but it is due to the causality of a.

Let us emphasize that our point is *not* that there is no distinction between x causing y and x and y being in mutual interaction. In the first example we saw that, even given the fact that if a acts on b and c, then it in turn is acted upon by b and c (even if in every case the cause interacts with the body that is affected), we can still make a distinction between what is due to the action of a upon b and c (in which case a is considered as cause) versus what is due to the interaction of b and c with a. Further, cases of "ongoing" interactions (Example 2 of the earth and the moon) can be distinguished from cases in which the interaction takes place at a particular time and continues (for a time) to have effects on both bodies. Our only point is that the distinction between causation and interaction (the two kinds of dynamical relations) cannot be correlated with determining succession and simultaneity (the two kinds of determination of time order) respectively.

We have been arguing as if the intent of the Second Analogy is to show that succession must be determined in terms of causality, whereas the intent of the Third Analogy is to show that simultaneity or coexistence must be determined in terms of mutual interaction. In other words, we have been arguing as if there is a division of labor between the Second Analogy (cause and effect) and the Third Analogy (mutual interaction) in dealing with the determination of succession and simultaneity or coexistence, respectively. This indeed seems to be Kant's intent as he introduces the Analogies by saying, "The three modes of time are *duration, succession,* and *coexistence.* There will, therefore, be three rules of all relations of appearances in time, and these rules will be prior to experience, and indeed make it possible" (CPR, B 219, p. 209). It seems natural to take Kant to be implying here that each relational category supplies a rule for determining appearances under one of the corresponding modes of time. The actual presentation of the Second and Third Analogies does not quite fit the intention expressed in this passage. It seems that the Second Analogy deals with the succession of states of one substance, whereas the Third Analogy deals with the coexistence of states of different substances. The question of the succession of a state of one substance upon a state of another substance is, seemingly, not considered. Let us note that in Case 1 of our first example we determine that b at p1 is simultaneous with c at p1′ (i.e., that states of different substances coexist) without reference to any interaction at all, but merely in reference to the causal action of some third substance (a). Thus even if we exclude the question of the succession of states in different substances, the kind of time-determination discussed in the Third Analogy (coexistence of states of different substances) cannot be peculiarly correlated with the dynamical relation discussed in the Third Analogy (mutual interaction). If we include (as we ought) the question of the succession of states of different substances, then this kind of time-determination cannot be peculiarly correlated with either of the dynamical relations (causality, mutual interaction) to the exclusion of the other.

16. Accidental Occurrences

1) Just after I walk out of my room, the faucet begins to drip.
2) Just at the time the faucet begins to drip the wind blows a vase

off the table. Here we have 1) a succession, and 2) a coexistence of states of affairs, respectively, which would ordinarily be characterized as accidental or coincidental. We shall first attempt to characterize the essential structure of cases of accidental occurrences. We shall then see whether these cases present an objection to Kant's claim that all occurrences are rule-governed.

Suppose (i) there are two apples *a* and *b* on a tree and that a severe wind comes along and blows both of them from the tree at the same time. Suppose (ii) that apple *a* after growing to a certain size exerts a great enough force on the twig it hangs from so that the twig is just about ready to break off. Suppose that a woodpecker pecks on the twig apple *b* hangs from, and just at the time that he pecks through the twig and apple *b* falls off the force exerted by apple *a* breaks its twig and apple *a* falls to the ground. The simultaneous occurrence of both apples *a* and *b* falling to the ground is an accidental occurrence in (ii) but is not accidental in (i).

The difference between (i) and (ii) is *not* that in the latter case there is a coincidence of conditions (or circumstances) without which the occurrence would not have happened, for there is a coincidence of relevant conditions in the former Case (i) also. The fact that the severe wind can cause *both* apples to fall from the tree simultaneously depends on a certain coincidence of initial conditions. For example, if apple *a* had been attached by a sturdier twig to the tree, the force of the wind might not have been sufficient to blow *a* off the tree. In Case (i), *one* initiating condition (the force of the wind) is the cause simultaneously of two occurrences (the falling of *a* and the falling of *b*), though the wind being able to effect both occurrences depends on certain conditions holding simultaneously at the time the wind exerts its force. In other words, there is a coincidence of *standing* initial conditions. In Case (ii), however, there is a coincidence of *initiating* conditions. The woodpecker pecks through the one twig (the initiating condition of the falling of apple *b*) at the same time that the downward force of apple *a* is sufficient to break the other twig (i.e., at the time this downward force becomes the initiating condition of the falling of apple *a*).

Case (i) is analogous to our example in the preceding section where billiard ball *a* hits both *b* and *c,* causing *b* and *c* simultaneously to move. If *b*'s mass had been so great as to resist any motion upon impact by *a* (i.e., if one of the "standing" conditions of the situation had been different) then the simultaneous motion of *b* and *c* would not have occurred. In other words, the simultaneous occurrence of two effects (the motion of *b* and the motion of *c*) depends on a "coincidence" (a coexistence) of standing conditions.

An analogue of Case (ii) would be the following *Case 3* (Fig. 5): Billiard ball *a* hits *b* at a certain time, causing *b* to move. At the time that *a* hits *b*, *c* hits *d*, causing *d* to move.

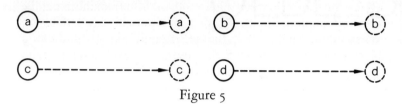

Figure 5

The motion of *b* takes place at the same time as the motion of *d*. Here we have a simultaneous occurrence that is traced back to two different initiating conditions (the impact of *a* and the impact of *c*).

Accidental occurrences are not restricted to the kind of case where *two* substances undergoing change of state are involved. Consider the following case. Billiard ball *a* hits billiard ball *b*, which begins to move. As it is moving, *b* is hit by *c* at a direction perpendicular to its line of motion whereupon *b*'s direction is altered:

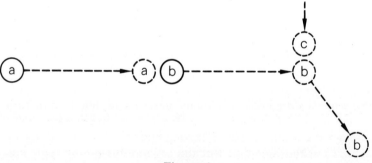

Figure 6

It is a coincidence that *a* should have hit *b* just at the time that *a*, causing *b* to move, brings *b* in the line of *c*'s motion, thereby enabling *c* to effect a further change of state in *b* (Fig. 6).

Another example of an accidental occurrence with effects in one substance would be the following: A batter hits a ball high into the air, though not very far. Just at the time the ball is in the air a strong wind comes along and carries the ball over the fence through the window of a neighboring house. The successive positions of the baseball from the time it leaves the bat to the time it hits the window can be accounted for according to laws, but only given the coincidence of two initiating conditions.

From these examples it seems that the coincidence involved in accidental occurrences is primarily the coincidence of different *initiating* conditions. Thus, in case (ii) the coincidence of both apples falling from the tree at the same time can be traced back to the coincidence of the two initiating conditions (*a* growing to a certain weight, and the woodpecker pecking at the twig from which apple *b* hangs). The coincidence of the effects is a simultaneous occurrence according to rules. We can understand, in accordance with causal rules and given the circumstances, why it should be that both apples fall to the ground simultaneously. What we do not understand (as I have presented the case) is why it should be that the woodpecker pecks through one twig just as the other apple grows to a certain weight (what we do not understand is why the given circumstances that enable us to determine the simultaneous falling of the apples in accordance with rules should themselves obtain or occur). Similarly, in Case 3, we can understand, in accordance with causal laws and given the coincidence of initiating conditions, why *b* should move simultaneously with *d*. Again, from the way we have presented the case, what we do not understand is why *a* should have hit *b* just at the time that *c* hit *d*. Given that *a* hit *b* just at the time that *c* hit *d,* the simultaneous motion of *b* and *d* is thoroughly determinable in accordance with causal laws. Similarly, *given* that the apple's weight becomes sufficient to break off one twig at the time the woodpecker pecked through the other, the simultaneous falling of the two apples is also determinable in accordance with rules.

Now what I wish to suggest is that an analogous situation obtains in cases of occurrences that we would not characterize as accidental. Let us take as a simple example Case 4, one billiard ball hitting another (Fig. 7). Given that *a* hits *b* with a certain impact and from a certain angle, the succession of *b* being at different positions $p_1, \ldots,$ pn is a succession in accordance with a rule L. L enables us to determine on the basis of certain conditions, one of which, the impact of *a,* is singled out as the initiating condition, the succession of states in *b*. Given certain conditions and the validity of L, the motion of

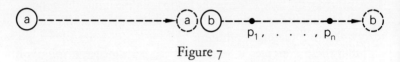

<figure>Figure 7</figure>

b "follows." Now notice that, so far, L itself does not determine that the initiating condition of its application should obtain or occur; the impact of *a* upon *b* is not determined by L. L determines the motion of *b*, given that the impact by *a* occurred. It does not, as far as this goes, determine that the impact of *a* should have occurred.

If we ask why *a* should have hit *b* at this time (just at the time it did rather than at some other time or not at all), this question is not answered by determining the motion of *b* in accordance with L, given that *a* hit *b*. From the fact that L does not itself determine that the impact occurred, it does not follow that the impact itself did not occur in accordance with a rule. We can state this point generally as follows: *In no case of determining a succession or simultaneity of states in accordance with a rule do we thereby determine why the conditions of applying the rule should obtain.* This is not to say that we could not *go on* to determine why the conditions of applying the rule should obtain in terms of some (perhaps the same) rule; only that determining why the conditions of applying the rule should obtain will necessarily introduce reference to still other conditions. For example, in the case at hand (Fig. 8), given that *a* is at rest at p1 and *b* is at rest at p2 and *c* hit *a* from a certain angle with a certain momentum, we can determine in accordance with L that *a* must hit *b* with a certain impact; i.e., we can determine in accordance with L that the exact impact of *a* upon *b* should occur (this impact

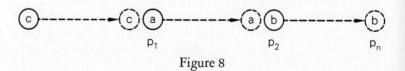

<figure>Figure 8</figure>

being in turn the condition of applying L to determine the succession of states in *b*).

In the case of the two apples falling from the tree simultaneously, given the coincidence of the initiating conditions, the falling of the apples is determined in accordance with rules. In other words, accidental occurrences (which follow from a coincidence of initiating conditions) are not to be distinguished by saying that in such occurrences something about the situation (viz., the coincidence of initiating conditions) is left undetermined. In any case of determining an occurrence in accordance with a rule something is left undetermined, viz., that the initiating condition of applying the rule should obtain or occur at that time. Why billiard ball *a* should have hit billiard ball *b* with such and such an impact at such and such a time is not answered by determining the succession of *b* according to L, for this determination proceeds on the assumption that it is given that *a* did hit *b* with this impact at this time.

Thus, there is nothing about the structure of cases of accidental occurrences (which always involve a coincidence of initiating conditions) that makes the occurrences any less determinable in accordance with rules. The only point of bringing up such cases as objections to the thoroughgoing determinability of occurrences according to rules seems to be that the coincidence of initiating conditions in such cases does not itself seem to be determinable in accordance with any obviously detectable rules. In other words, it seems that in these cases we could not go on and determine why the initiating conditions should have obtained simultaneously. Kant's claim is that there must be some condition such that, given this condition, the simultaneity of, say, the one apple exerting a certain force with the woodpecker pecking through a twig can be determined in accordance with some rule. What this rule might be (and what this condition of applying the rule might be) is not at all obvious. In Case 4, one billiard ball *a* hitting another *b* (a nonaccidental occurrence), Kant's claim would be there must be some condition such that, given this condition, the impact of *a* upon *b* can be determined to occur in accordance with a rule. Now in this case we have some idea that the rule will be a law of motion and that the condition of applying the rule will be the exertion of some force. In other words, the only objection to the case of the two apples is that we have only the vaguest idea (if any idea at all) what the rules (and thus what the conditions of applying the rules) for determining the coincidence of the two occurrences (the pecking of the woodpecker and the exertion of a certain force by an apple) might be. The fact that the rules and conditions are not obvious in this case does not derive primarily from the fact that this is an accidental occurrence. In our previous example (Case 3) of billiard ball *a* hitting *b* just at the time that *c* hit *d* (an accidental occurrence), we do have an idea that the rule for determining the simultaneity of the impacts will be laws of motion and that the initiating condition will be the exertion of some force. Thus, the objection seems to be that in some occurrences the rule in accordance with which the occurrence can be determined is not obviously forthcoming. This objection must be divorced from the distinction between accidental versus nonaccidental occurrences. Thus, it is not at all obvious why a woodpecker should peck at a twig when it does (the causal rules in accordance with which animals act are not obviously detectable), but a woodpecker pecking at a twig is not in itself an accidental (coincidental) occurrence.

Now Kant's claim is not that all succession or simultaneity can be determined in accordance with obviously or easily detectable rules. He is not claiming that we have any more than the vaguest idea (if any idea at all) of what the rules (and thus the conditions of applying the rules) might be in terms of which we could determine the particular occurrence. This being so, cases such as the one of the two apples are not in themselves an objection to Kant's claim.

In attempting to mark off accidental occurrences as occurrences involving a coincidence of initiating conditions, we have glossed over the rationale for the distinction between initiating conditions and other initial conditions (standing conditions). The characterization given, viz., that an initiating condition is one that determines whether the event takes place at all, whereas a standing condition determines merely the exact character of the event that takes place, will not do. For example, if the apple on the twig had weighed less and thus had exerted a lesser force (i.e., if this "standing" condition had been different) the event, the falling of the apple, might not have taken place at all when the wind blew.

We might attempt to characterize the difference as follows: the initiating condition is the change in the situation just prior to the event. If the wind had not blown at that time there would have been no change in the situation, or at least no swift or sudden change; the increment in mass of the apple is too slow to count as a noticeable alteration in the situation just prior to the event. This characterization will not do for the following reason. Suppose no wind came along and the apple continued to grow until, under the weight of the apple, the twig snapped. Here I think we would single out the weight of the apple as the initiating condition (the cause) of the event, yet there was no swift or noticeable alteration in the weight of the apple just prior to the event.

A better characterization, I think, is the following. All initial conditions other than the wind could have been predicted or accounted for on the basis of *similar* preceding conditions; i.e., the other conditions are taken as parameters of the situation. In the case of the movement of the planets, all conditions are parameters in this sense; i.e., the position of the planets at any time is a function of their mass and position at other times. The conditions in this case form a *closed* system. A closed system is one in which all initial conditions for applying a law are themselves accountable in terms of this law applied to further "similar" initial conditions. More precisely, a closed system is one whose description at a certain time is governable by laws whose conditions of application constitute a description of the system at some other time. The system is describable in terms of determinables and alterations in the system are different determinations of these determinables.

Consider again the case of a billiard ball *a* hitting a second billiard ball *b* that moves until it happens to be hit by another billiard ball *c* (Fig. 9).

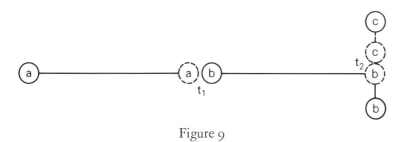

Figure 9

It is, we said, a coincidence that *a* should have hit *b* at such a time to bring *b* within the range of *c*. The Law L governing *a*'s impact upon *b* is the same as that governing *c*'s impact upon *b,* and the initial conditions of applying L in the two cases are "similar" (mass, velocity, angle of collision, etc.). And yet if we think of *a* hitting *b* and *c* hitting *b* as a system, it is not a closed system. The reason is as follows. The application of L to *c*'s impact upon *b* (the system at t_2) includes certain initial conditions of *c* (position, mass, velocity, etc.) that are *not* initial conditions of applying L to *a*'s impact upon *b*; i.e., they are not part of the description of the system at t_1 (because where *c* is and how fast it is moving, etc., is irrelevant to applying L at t_1 to *a*'s impact upon *b*). In other words, *c*'s position, velocity, are new parameters, parameters that are not relevant to the application of L to the system until time t_2. It is not enough then that the changes in a system be determined by different applications of the same law under "similar" conditions of applying the law. To have a closed system the conditions of applying the law relevant to one stage of the system must be relevant to applying the governing law at any other stage of the system.

This account of what constitutes a closed system is vague, but the connection between closed systems and the singling out of initiating conditions is, I think, quite precise. An initiating condition is a condition that breaks up a closed system. A closed system can be broken up in two ways; by the introduction of extraneous (nonparametric) conditions or by the "playing out" of the closed system itself. An example of the former would be a wind coming along whereupon an apple falls from a tree. The apple growing on the twig forms a closed system (approximately, anyway, if we include soil-type, average rainfall, etc.) in which the weight of the apple, the tension in the twig, and so on, are determinable via mechanical and botanical laws. The wind breaks up this closed system of the growth of an apple and the tension exerted on a twig. A better example would be the intrusion into our solar system of a mass sufficient in size to disrupt the "ordinary" course of the planets around the sun. Examples of a closed system playing itself out would be an apple growing to sufficient size to break the twig by its own weight, or the masses of the solar system, say, eventually losing gravitational energy until the planets collapse into the sun. In both cases, I suggest, we would single out as initiating conditions the parameters of the system.

Let us make a distinction between deterministic and indeterministic applications of a law. A deterministic application is an application of a law to changes within a closed system, while an indeterministic application is an application of a law to an opening up of a closed system. The application of Newton's law of gravitation to the ordinary course of the solar system would be a deterministic application.

Newton's law also explains what would result if a large mass intruded upon the ordinary course of the solar system. In this case the law of gravitation would be applied indeterministically. In deterministic applications of a law no initiating conditions are singled out; in indeterministic applications an initiating condition is always singled out (either as the intrusion of an extraneous factor into the closed system or as the last state of a closed system playing itself out). Accidental occurrences, then, involving a coincidence of initiating conditions, are a subclass of indeterministic applications of law.

Note that in the sense in which I use the terms, "deterministic" and "indeterministic" characterize applications of laws, not laws themselves (one and the same law may apply in either way depending on the circumstances), and "indeterministic" does not mean ungoverned by laws. A derivative use of these terms would be that the universe is deterministic if all events are governed by laws that, in all cases, apply deterministically. Another way of putting this is to say that the universe is deterministic if the totality of events constitute a closed system with respect to the laws governing the universe. It is not true that a universe completely governed by laws must therefore be deterministic. Suppose the entire universe consisted of those three billiard balls *a, b, c,* and of *a* hitting *b* just at the time to bring *b* with the range of *c* (Fig. 10).

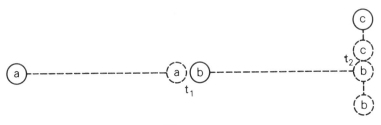

Figure 10

It is true that, given the state of the universe at time t_1, its state at any other time is completely determinable in accordance with the laws of mechanics. And yet this universe does not, as we have indicated, form a closed system, for part of the state of the universe at t_1 includes certain conditions regarding *c* that are extraneous relative to applying the laws of mechanics to *a*'s impact upon *b* at t_1 and are introduced as *new* parameters in applying the laws to c's impact upon b at t_2. Such a universe, though thoroughly governable by mechanical laws, would not be deterministic as would a universe consisting solely of the planetary masses and the sun interacting according to gravitational laws.

The question of determinism *versus* indeterminism is usually regarded as being relevant to questions of freedom and action. Let me simply indicate that according to my use of these terms the relevance would lie in investigating some such claim as the following: Human actions are always intrusions upon the "physical" world (the world as governed by laws of physical sciences); they are not (cannot be) incorporated as parameters of closed physical systems.

The interesting distinction is between deterministic and indeterministic applications of law, not between accidental and nonaccidental occurrences. Kant's claim in the Analogies is not, in any case, that all events must be subject to laws that apply in all cases deterministically. Being able to trace the connection between events via laws does not presuppose that these events constitute a closed system, nor that these events are part of some larger closed system.

In summary:

> 1) An accidental occurrence involves a coincidence of initiating conditions.
>
> 2) Given that the initiating conditions obtain at the time they do, the occurrence (resulting from these conditions) is determinable in accordance with rules.
>
> 3) It is no objection to say that the coincidence of initiating conditions is not itself determined in determining what follows, *given* that this coincidence of initiating conditions occurs. The same is true in cases of indeterministic, nonaccidental occurrences, where the occurrence of the one initiating condition is not ipso facto determined in determining what follows, given that this initiating condition occurs.
>
> 4) Nor is it an objection to say that the coincidence of initiating conditions does not occur in accordance with any obviously detectable rules.
>
>> a) This lack of obvious rules is not specific to accidental occurrences.
>>
>> b) Kant's claim is not that the rules in accordance

with which occurrences obtain must be obviously forthcoming.

17. *Teleological Judgment*

In the *Critique of Judgment* Kant argues for the necessity of teleology in explaining organized beings. Teleology, according to Kant, cannot be "reduced to" mechanical laws. "Now this concept [natural purposes] brings the reason into a quite different order of things from that of a mere mechanism of nature, which is no longer satisfying here" (*Critique of Judgment,* hereafter CJ; § 66, p. 223). This seems incompatible with the judgment of the Second Analogy if we take that argument to have established the universal applicability of mechanical laws.

One way to attempt to avoid the contradiction is to say that although all phenomena are governable by mechanical laws, some phenomena are also governable by teleological laws, leaving aside the serious question of how the same phenomena can be governed by conflicting kinds of laws. Certain of Kant's remarks, however, preclude following up this way of avoiding the contradiction. He says that we should investigate phenomena according to mechanical laws "as far as we can" (CJ, § 70, p. 235). Here Kant seems explicitly to be calling into question the universal applicability of mechanical laws. We have, then, before us the following questions:

  1. In what domain and why are teleological laws required at all?

  2. In what sense are teleological laws irreducible to or of a different order than mechanical laws?

  3. How is the requirement for teleological laws and their irreducibility to mechanical laws itself compatible with the universal applicability of mechanical laws?

The answer to all three questions depends, I think, on making a distinction between the function of causal laws as rules of time-determination and their function in explanations. What has been established in the Second Analogy is that there can be no gaps in determinability of time position and hence no gap in the applicability of rules for determining such position. What has not been established in the Second Analogy (for the reason that it is not a constitutive condition of the possibility of experience) is that there can be no gaps in understanding or explaining phenomena. Mechanical laws do not suffice for complete explanations, although such laws do and must suffice for complete determinability of time position.

Kant represents the antinomy of judgment as, on the one hand, ". . . all production of material things and their forms must be judged to be possible according to merely mechanical laws," while, on the other hand, ". . . some products of material nature cannot be judged to be possible according to merely mechanical laws" (CJ, § 70, p. 234). His resolution of the antinomy is that both the thesis and the antithesis are to be construed as regulative, not constitutive, principles; as principles of the reflexive, not the determinant, judgment (CJ, § 70, p. 234; see also p. 129, below). Regulative principles, however, are principles that guide us in understanding or explaining phenomena, not in determining their time-position. Kant explicitly characterizes the two maxims of the antinomy as two "methods of explanation" (CJ, § 71, p. 236; see also § 78, p. 260), as opposed to two methods of time-determination. The mechanical (or physical or natural or *nexus effectivus*) has not been shown in the Second Analogy to be the exclusive principle of explanation, or the necessary and sufficient means of understanding phenomena; it has been shown to be the universal principle of time-determination. How far phenomena can be understood, beyond what is required for them to be objects of judgment at all, is not something that can be determined a priori and is not something that has been determined in the Second Analogy. What methods of explanation are required in Reason's attempt at complete understanding is left open by the argument of the Second Analogy. The resolution of the apparent contradiction between the Second Analogy and the *Critique of Judgment* (the answer to question 3 above) is then this: The teleological principle is a required principle of *explanation* irreducible to mechanical laws, but all this is compatible with the universal applicability of the latter as rules determinant of time-position.

This suggested resolution commits Kant to the view that explaining or understanding phenomena is something more than being able to determine their time-positions according to mechanical laws. It commits him to the view that thoroughgoing time-determination according to mechanical laws is something less than thoroughgoing understanding or comprehensibility. Some account of what this something more is, is called for.

There are two major strands running through the *Critique of*

Judgment: a) the general purposiveness of nature in that particular empirical laws should be incorporable into a coherent system of laws, and *b*) the particular purposiveness of nature revealed in certain specific natural systems (in organized beings). Both strands may be regarded as accounts of what more would be involved in understanding phenomena than their time-position being determinable according to laws. Along the lines of *a,* understanding is something more than determinability of time-position in accordance with laws, for Reason requires that these laws themselves be integrated into a connected system. Along the lines of *b,* certain special phenomena cannot be understood nonteleologically. We can bypass a discussion of *a* since there ought to be no apparent discrepancy between *a* and the argument of the Second Analogy and since it has become quite commonplace (if not quite clear) that integrated systems of laws (theories) are the locus of scientific understanding.

With respect to *b* we are left with the following reformulations of questions 1 and 2 above:

1′ In what domain and why is the teleological method of explanation required?

2′ Why and how is it that the teleological method of explanation cannot be replaced by mechanical explanation? The answers to 1′ and 2′ ought also to make clearer how the irreplaceability of teleology is itself compatible with the universal applicability of mechanical laws as the means of determining time-position. What ought to be made clearer, that is, is how teleology can be an alternative method of explanation without at the same time being an alternative method of time-determination; how teleology can fill gaps in understanding where there are no gaps in time-determination according to laws.

We saw in the preceding section that a number of events may each be governable by mechanical laws (or by the same mechanical law), and yet the concurrence of the events may still be "accidental." This, I think, gives us a substantial clue as to the characterization of what sort of understanding is involved in teleological explanation. Given a concurrence of events $e_1, \ldots, e_n$, each is determinable in accordance with effective causal laws (either the same or different ones) and sets of initial conditions for applying the laws, so that we understand why each event occurred when it did; and yet we still seem predisposed to ask why they all should have occurred together. However odd, the concurrence of the events seems not to be satisfactorily explained by joint explanations of the individual occurrences; i.e., the concurrence still remains contingent (accidental) relative to the joint explanations of the different occurrences. How could it be that a separate explanation of why each of $e_1, \ldots e_n$ occurred when they did is not ipso facto an explanation of why they all occurred together? What is being called for by the latter that is not being supplied by the former? The answer, I suggest, is that in asking for a further explanation of the concurrence, we are asking that the explanation not itself involve unexplained joint occurrences. We are calling for the complete removal of coincidence or accidental collocation. Kant says, "When, e.g., we adduce the structure of a bird, the hollowness of its bones, the disposition of its wings for motion and of its tail for steering, etc., we say that all this is contingent in the highest degree according to the mere *nexus effectivus* of nature, without calling in the aid of a particular kind of causality, namely that of purpose *(nexus finalis)*" (CJ, § 61, p. 206). Explaining why each of $e_1, \ldots ,e_n$ occurred when it did in terms of one or more effective laws depends on a concurrence of initiating conditions in applying this law (or these laws) and so does not completely remove the factor of coincidence.

It seems prima facie that there are three different ways of eliminating coincidence in the explanandum without thereby shifting it to the explanans:

a) explanation in terms of conscious intent or purpose, or aesthetic explanation,

b) mechanical explanations that do not finally rest on a concurrence of initiating conditions, and

c) teleological explanations.

We can ask of a painting how it came to be that the colors and shapes are disposed on the canvas in such and such a way. Why a dark red sphere here and a streak of orange there? We may suppose that a complete mechanical explanation in terms of the muscle movements of the artist is, in principle, at hand. This type of explanation will not automatically remove contingency for there is no indication why the muscular movements that initiated the application of the red paint and the muscular movements that effected the streak should *both* have occurred. In asking about the disposition of the colors we are asking for a description of the structure of the painting, the interrelationships of the parts as they contribute to the structure. In a sense, we rather work backward, for given the structural description of the painting, we have then answered the question of why both series of muscular movements occurred. If we take this view of explanations in terms of purpose and intent, that they are really descriptions of structure and organization, then it is clear how such explanations eliminate coincidence, for what lies behind such description is that no part of the structure can be understood without bringing in the whole. In terms of such structural description, the situation does not arise that we antecedently understand why the red and why the orange and then call for an explanation of why both, for what counts as understanding each part precisely precludes this. We are satisfied that we understand the structure only when we are satisfied that we have eliminated coincidence; i.e., when we are satisfied that understanding any part requires understanding the whole.

In any case, aesthetic understanding seems more a matter of appreciation than explanation. Part of the reason for this perhaps is that the element of time-determination is completely lacking here. It is irrelevant to the understanding of the painting which parts were completed first. The goal in understanding the painting would, in fact, seem to be to make any form of time-determination irrelevant. To say that no part can be understood except through the conception of the whole is to say you can start anywhere. This lack of relevance of time-determination can be brought out by the way in which we, as I have called it, work backward. The structural description of the painting "explains" why both muscular movements, but not why one before the other.

The second way of eliminating contingency is to trace the coincidence back through laws of effective causation until we reach a point where no coincidence of initiating conditions is required in applying the laws. Thus, the host of coincidences involved in the multiple collisions of all the billiard balls on a billiard table can be traced back to the original break by the cue. There are two points to observe about such explanations. First, it seems that tracing the occurrences back in this way is the only means of removing the contingency. The various collisions of the billiard balls, although they obey mechanical laws, seem random and seem not to have any structure apart from the origination. This differentiates this case from both the aesthetic and teleological cases. Second, there is no a priori reason to think that the contingency of all concurrences is eliminable in this way. Even in a universe thoroughly governable by mechanical laws, in tracing back a concurrence of events, each in accordance with mechanical laws, it may be that we never reach a point where the application of these laws no longer depends on a coincidence of initiating conditions.

The third way of alleviating coincidence is by means of the teleological method. Teleological explanation shares with artistic appreciation the central importance of the notion of structure or organization. Kant says, "For a thing to be a natural purpose, in the first place it is requisite that its parts (as regards their presence and their form) are only possible through their reference to the whole" (CJ, § 65, p. 219). Unlike the aesthetic case, the organization is dynamical as well as structural. ". . . it is requisite, secondly, that its parts should so combine in the unity of the whole that they are reciprocally cause and effect of each other's form" (CJ, § 65, pp. 219–20). Teleological explanation removes contingency not by tracing the parts back to a single cause, but by uniting them in the concept of a dynamical organization. As in the aesthetic case the parts are understood only in reference to the whole and so the contingency of the concurrence of the functioning parts is removed without having to separately trace them to a common originating cause.

Unlike the aesthetic case, in teleological explanation the mechanical redescription of how the parts perform their role in the organization of the whole does lead to a greater understanding. It must be noted, however, that such mechanical (physical and chemical) redescription does not eliminate the teleological character of the explanation. The explanation of the eye in terms of its functional value to the organism is not replaced but rather refined or made precise by a physical-chemical description of how the eye performs its sensory function. The dependency of the eye performing this function on other parts of the organism is again not removed but made more intricate and detailed by a physical description of, say, the control and interpretative mechanisms of the brain. To say otherwise would be like saying that a mechanical understanding of how a thermostat works eliminates its self-regulative structure. Teleological explanations as such are not provisional to mechanical explanations, but teleological explanations couched in vague terms such as sensation, digestion, and so on, are provisional to teleological explanations framed in precise physical redescriptions of these terms.

Teleological explanation is not an alternative to mechanical explanation in the sense that explanation in terms of nonphysical agencies would be an alternative. Rather, they are a type of rule instructing us in the joint application of mechanical laws. Mechanical laws are not to be applied in the explanation of the eye without also being applied to the brain. We can gain some insight into the way in which teleological explanations function as such instructions by the way they relate to time-determination. We saw in the aesthetic case that time-determination is irrelevant in "working backward." This is unlike the teleological case where we say such things as that only an organism whose brain was developing in such and such a way would be developing such and such sense organs, or that only an organism with a certain mechanical dexterity of the thumb and forefinger would have (need of or could make use of) such and such a development of the brain. Nothing in these phrases points to any sort of nonphysical development. Rather, they are instructions that the origination of certain parts are to be physically explained only in conjunction with the physical explanation of other parts, the principle behind the instruction being the functional interdependence of the working parts in relation to the integrity of the organism.

Teleological explanations coordinate what would otherwise be the unrelated application of one or more mechanical laws. In *this* regard they are analogous to a rule to the effect that in applying the gravitational law to the motion of a particular planet the solar system as a whole is to be taken as a unit of application. To say that in understanding the motion of any one planet the motion of the others cannot be disregarded is not to augment the law of gravitation by another law, but rather to instruct in the application of the gravitational law. We can begin to see, I think, how rules instructing joint application diverge from explanations in terms of single originating causes by the failure of the maxim: Apply laws jointly to any group of elements with a single origin. If the solar system originated in a fragmentation of the sun and if it were possible for some fragments to have escaped the solar gravitational attraction, these fragments would share a common origin with the planets, but they would not be included when applying gravitational laws to determine the motion of a planet. A disanalogy between the planetary system and natural organisms is that in the former case the form of the law of gravity itself (an inverse square law) delineates the structure of what is to count as a system of joint application (viz., only masses large enough in proportion to their distances matter), whereas in the latter case, the physical and chemical laws do not prescribe, even in outline form, what the structure of the joint system of application would be.

We may now summarize each of the three different means of eliminating contingency and then give a final answer to questions 1′ and 2′, above:*

> a) Aesthetic organization eliminates contingency of concurrence by precluding any separate understanding (appreciation) of the parts.

> b) Mechanical tracing eliminates contingency of concurrence by deriving the concurrence from a single originating cause.

> c) Teleological explanation eliminates contingency by prescribing rules for the joint application of physical laws on the principle of the functional interdependence of the parts of an open system.

> 1′. Teleological explanation is thus required for the elimination of contingent concurrence in the application of physical laws to certain kinds of systems. In this sense it has an important role to play in the way scientific laws are employed in understanding phenomena.

> 2′. In one sense teleology is incommensurate with the application of mechanical laws, for it consists in second-order rules of when and how the former laws are to be applied jointly; it is not itself a *competing* law to be applied. In another sense teleology is an alternative to the mechanical tracing method of eliminating contingency in that the principle behind the instructed joint application is the interdependent structure of the elements, not their traceability to a common original cause.

The genus of teleological explanation is the removal of contingency. The differentia is the way in which it removes such

---

* See p. 123, above.

contingency, namely, as being a set of instructions for the joint application of one or more laws to otherwise disparate elements. Further, these instructions are based on the organization of the elements according to dynamical functional interdependence. Perhaps, then, it should be clearer how the teleological method of explanation (as a method of application of laws) can fill in gaps in understanding where there are no gaps in time-determination. A set of instructions for the joint application of a law or laws to different elements neither fills in nor contravenes the time-position of these elements as determined by the law or laws separately.

Perhaps, too, we can more precisely characterize the point of Kant's including both strands in the *Critique of Judgment*.* Both the general and specific purposiveness or organization of nature relate to our desire for understanding phenomena. This desire is not satisfied by the universality of time-determination, which is a constitutive principle of the possibility of phenomena, not a completion of the task of explaining them. Both kinds of purposiveness are related to understanding or explanation through the removal of contingency; the general removes the contingency of the different specific laws themselves by uniting the laws into a system of laws (theory), while the specific purposiveness removes the contingency of different applications of a single law or different laws (i.e., applications of a law or laws to separate elements) by uniting the elements into an organized system. Both strands can be understood as matters for the *reflective* judgment in that they both, in their different ways, systematize and regulate empirical laws and their applications, rather than apply to objects directly.

Finally, we can perhaps better understand Kant's resolution of the antinomy of judgment. Kant's resolution has been taken by H. W. Cassirer (1938, pp. 345–46, 351–52) to be ambiguous in the following two statements:

> *a*) Both teleology and mechanism are principles of the reflective judgment that have been mistaken for constitutive principles.

> *b*) Mechanism is a constitutive principle, teleology, on the other hand, is a merely regulative principle that has been mistaken for a constitutive principle.

---

* See pp. 122–23, above.

The difference is that in *a* mechanism is said to be regulative, whereas in *b* it remains constitutive. Supporting *a,* Kant says of the mechanistic principle, "All that is implied is: I *must* always *reflect* upon them [events in nature] *according to the principle* of the mere mechanism of nature" (CJ, § 70, p. 234). Supporting *b,* according to Cassirer, is the argument of the Second Analogy that makes effective causality a constitutive principle, and the following passage:

> All appearance of an antinomy between the maxims of the proper physical (mechanical) and the teleological (technical) methods of explanation rests therefore on this that we [in each case?] confuse a fundamental proposition of the reflective with one of the determinant judgment, and the *autonomy* of the first [reflective judgment] (which has mere subjective validity for our use of reason in respect of particular empirical laws) with the *heteronomy* of the second [determinant judgment] which must regulate itself according to laws (universal or particular) given to it by the understanding (CJ, § 71, p. 236).

It seems to me that this passage by itself is in no way clear support for *b* and can be read (as I have bracketed it) quite well as being in conformity with *a*; i.e., as saying that both methods of explanation (both maxims) have been mistaken for propositions of the determinant judgment. Second and more important, *a* is not, as we have seen, incompatible with the argument of the Second Analogy, for the mechanical method of *explanation* (removing contingency of concurrence by tracing events back through *nexus effectivus* to a single originating cause) has nowhere been established as a constitutive principle of nature. The mechanical tracing method, insofar as it instructs us in, or regulates, *the use* of mechanical laws to eliminate contingency, is easily enough understood as a regulative principle or a principle of the reflective judgment.

18. Necessity and Universality

Kant seems to hold that a causal connection is, in some sense, a necessary and universal connection. He says,

> For this concept [causality] makes the strict demand that something A should be such that something B follows

from it *necessarily and in accordance with some universal rule.* Appearances do indeed present cases from which a [specific] rule can be obtained, according to which something usually happens, but they never prove the sequence to be *necessary.* To the synthesis of cause [A] and effect [B] there belongs a dignity which cannot be empirically expressed, namely, that the effect not only succeeds upon the cause, but that it is posited *through* it and arises *out* of it. This strict universality is never characteristic of empirical rules; they can acquire through induction only comparative universality (CPR, A 91, B 124, p. 125).

Again he says,

Experience does indeed show that one appearance customarily follows upon another, but not that this sequence is necessary, nor that we can argue *a priori* and with complete universality from the antecedent, viewed as a condition, to the consequent (CPR, A 112, p. 139).

And in the *Prolegomena* he says,

The concept of cause implies a rule, according to which one state follows another necessarily; but experience can only show us that one state of things often, or at most, commonly follows another, and therefore affords neither strict universality, nor necessity (P, p. 76).

Thus, in some sense Kant holds that *particular* causal connections are necessary and universal. By this he does not mean that we can know a priori what, in particular cases, causes what (in this he agrees with Hume). We can only determine empirically what causes what, where the empirical criterion of, say, x being the cause of y is that x is always present when y occurs. He holds that *in* determining (empirically) that x is the cause of y, *what it is that we are determining* is (at least) that y universally and necessarily obtains, given x. Given x, y must occur (except for "interfering conditions"; there will always be some mitigating explanation if y does not occur on a certain occasion, given x).

All I can learn from experience is that, given x, y usually occurs or that y has always occurred when x occurred in the past. We take this conjunction as an empirical criterion of a *causal* connection;

i.e., we assert on the basis of our experience of a constant conjunction of x and y, that x is the cause of y, which is to say that, given x, y necessarily and universally (not just commonly) occurs. This assertion goes beyond what we could have learned from experience, though it is based on experience.

The point is, for Hume, we are only justified in asserting that, given x, y has always occurred in our experience. For Kant, we are justified in asserting that, given x, y must always obtain (not just at times in the past when we have actually experienced y), *if* indeed x is the cause of y. Now we can never be sure that we have got it right that x is the cause of y. There is always the possibility that y will not occur even given that x occurred, with no plausible mitigating explanation. We may, after more careful scrutiny, conclude that z occurred in all cases in which y occurred including cases where y occurred without x occurring. We may thus conclude that z, not x, is the condition of the occurrence of y. But whatever the specific cause of y turns out to be (though this can only be determined empirically and is subject to correction), that cause is necessarily and universally connected with y. Kant says in the *Prolegomena,*

> But how does this proposition, "that judgments of experience contain necessity in the synthesis of perceptions," agree with my statement so often before inculcated, that "experience as cognition *a posteriori* can afford contingent judgments only"? When I say that experience teaches me something, I mean only the perception that lies in experience,—for example, that heat always follows the shining of the sun on a stone [i.e., I always perceive one to occur when the other is present]; consequently, the proposition of experience is always so far accidental. *That this heat necessarily follows upon the shining of the sun* is contained indeed in the judgment of experience [by means of the concept of cause] yet it is a fact not learned by experience [unless we are prepared to *take* constant conjunctions as evidence for *causal* connections] . . . (P, p. 63 n.)

The claim that particular causal connections are necessary and universal is perfectly compatible with the claim that we can only empirically ascertain which particular causal connections obtain. *If* x is the cause of y, then y necessarily and universally occurs, given

x. This is not to say that it is necessary that x (as opposed to z, say) is the cause or the condition of y occurring. It is this latter claim only that would conflict with the statement that we cannot know a priori what causes what.

Lovejoy argues that Kant's reply to Hume fails unless Kant can prove *a*) if x and y have been conjoined in my experience then they will always (continue in the future to) be conjoined. (Lovejoy, 1906; in Gram, 1967). This however, is to confuse the problem of the validation of our inductive knowledge with the question of whether or not there are causal connections in nature. Hume argued both 1) that there are difficulties in basing our knowledge of the future on our knowledge of the past, and 2) that there are difficulties in the very concept of a causal (necessary and universal) connection. Kant is primarily concerned with 2; i.e., to show that the concept of a necessary connection is not subject to the difficulties Hume claimed. An answer to 1 would require that we can necessarily ascertain correctly what causes what, while an answer to 2 requires a filling in of what constitutes a necessary connection. It is not Lovejoy's *a* that Kant needs to establish, but rather *b,* if x is the cause of y, then y is universally and necessarily connected to x. The argument for *b* turns on the fact that we determine appearances as successive on the basis of rules; it hinges on the *function* or *use* of rules in our experience. It is to this argument that we now proceed.

It has been shown in section 12 that causal laws, laws that enable us to infer temporal ordering based on features of experience, must be employed in experience. We have now to see how it has thereby been shown that the concept of causality, in the full-fledged sense in which it involves necessity and universality of connection, must be employed in experience.

Kant's claim may be put as follows: Causal laws are rules that license inferences from features of events to the temporal ordering of events ("inference tickets" in Ryle's terminology). When we determine the temporal order of events in terms of a causal law, we are using the law as a license. Now suppose M is a causal law used to determine the order of certain events (based on features of the events and "surrounding" circumstances); i.e., suppose M is that rule in terms of which we make the transition from 1) x being P1 and y being P2 (and certain other relevant features of the situation obtaining, where what is *relevant* is delineated by M) to 2) x being prior (or posterior, as the case may be) to y. Now the particular order of succession, x-y say, is one of the instances of M in the sense that M asserts or implies that, given certain circumstances and given the nature of x and y, x shall precede y. In other words, if under these conditions y should have preceded x, this would be a disconfirmation of M. Now the point is there is a sense in which given the situation and the relevant aspects of x and y, y *could not be determined* to have preceded x (i.e., a sense in which x must be determined to have preceded y) because we determine (we are granting) the order of succession of x and y in terms of M. If the order of x and y in the relevant circumstances is determined by M, then the order of x and y must be determined to be what M asserts it to be. M cannot be determined as failing to hold in any particular case for which it is the rule in terms of which the order of events in that case is determined by us. M can only fail in a certain case if the succession of events in that case does not agree with what M asserts or implies it to be, but this failure of agreement cannot arise, since the order of the event is determined by us precisely in terms of what M asserts or implies it to be (i.e., the order of the succession, granted that it is determined in terms of M, can only be determined to be what M asserts or implies it to be).

For example, when we determine the date of the fossilized remains of an animal (*when* the animal's remains were imprinted) on the basis of certain geological laws, these laws are being employed as licenses or inference tickets. Given certain circumstances, these laws imply that the imprinting took place at a certain time *t*. Now the point is, if we are determining when the imprinting took place solely on the basis of these laws, then we cannot determine the imprinting to have taken place at any time other than *t*. In this sense these laws, *qua employed as licenses,* necessarily apply to all cases for which they are employed in such a way. *No* succession of states of affairs or events can be determined as failing to take place in accordance with that law (or those laws) in terms of which the order of succession is determined by us in the first place. In a sense, when a particular law L is employed by us to determine the temporal order of events *e1* and *e2, it is not the law that conforms to the order of* e1 *and* e2, *but rather the determination of the order of* e1 *and* e2 *that conforms (that must conform) to the law.* In this way the necessity and universality of causal laws derives from their *use* as licenses in terms of which we determine temporal order. This does not imply that it is necessary that L (as opposed to M) should be the (or a) rule in terms of which we determine temporal order. *Which* rules are (justifiably) employed as licenses is ascertained empirically on the basis of experience. This does not contradict the fact that once (and as long as) we employ a rule as such a license for inferring temporal order, the temporal order inferred will be precisely what the rule asserts or implies it to be.

That a subject is committed to using a rule as an inference ticket and that the subject takes the rule as supporting counterfactual conditionals are two sides of the same coin. In this way, the necessity and universality of causal connections (as licenses for inferring temporal order) is linked to the *epistemic* aspect of the concept of causality, viz., that it applies to objects only for a subject who judges of objects under the nonmaterial hypothetical form of judgment.* Thus, in the Second Analogy it is shown that the full-fledged concept of causality (as involving necessity and universality and as being an epistemic notion related to the nonmaterial hypothetical form of judgment) must be employed if time-determination, and thus if judging about what is given in experience and thus, ultimately, if a form of consciousness in which the subject can distinguish himself from what is given to him, is to be possible.

---

* The remarks in this section apply equally, I think, in the case of probabilistic laws. Probabilistic laws too may be employed to determine time-position and their being so employable is what distinguishes them as laws. The element of probability does not obfuscate the difference between causal laws (probable or not) on the one hand and mere generalizations on the other. Even probabilistic laws must support counterfactuals (such as if x had occurred y *probably would have* occurred), and herein lies the element of necessity and universality of such laws side by side with the element of probability.

4   *Transcendental Idealism*

The various doctrines constituting transcendental idealism are, according to Kant, essentially bound up with the possibility of a priori knowledge and the possibility of experience. What I propose to do is to determine what idealistic implications are implicit in Kant's theories of space and time, the categories, and judgment as these theories have been presented above. I propose to determine what sort of idealism is demanded by or naturally rises out of Kant's analysis of experience. I hope to convince the reader that each of the following tenets derives inevitably from Kant's basic insights into the structure of experience:

a) The subject is the source of unity in experience or the subject contributes certain elements to experience.

b) The subject can contribute elements to experience only because what he has to deal with are not things in themselves.

c) The categories are not concepts of (or concepts applying to) things in themselves.

d) Transcendental idealism is compatible with empirical realism. It is the transcendental realist who is led to adopt empirical idealism.

e) Space and time are not things or properties of things; they are mere forms of intuition, and what is in space and time are not things in themselves.

Kant takes himself to have established transcendental idealism in the Aesthetic though he returns to the doctrine again in various sections of the Analytic. We shall begin by discussing the doctrine in relation to space and time. A real comprehension of the doctrine, however, is to be found in relation to the categories so that the discussion with respect to space and time must be taken as provisional until we return to it in light of the doctrine as presented in the Analytic.

19. Preliminary Indications

As stated in the Aesthetic, the doctrine of transcendental idealism is that all that is given in space and time are appearances or representations because space and time are not objective but mere forms of intuition. If we understand "appearances" or representations" in a Berkeleian sense as modifications of individual minds, it is not at all clear how the ideality of what is given in space and time (the characterization of what is given in space and time as appearance) follows from the ideality of space and time. Kant is quite insistent that there can be only one space and time. The notion of individuals each with their own private space and time is quite foreign to Kant's thought. Space and time are forms of our intuition collectively, not each one of our forms of intuition individually. If this is so, it is hard to see how it follows from the fact that we apprehend spatially and temporally that what each one of us thus apprehends spatially and temporally are mere modifications of each of our individual minds.

What distinguishes sensibility from understanding is that the former is passive and is in immediate relation to the singular. When Kant says that space and time are forms of intuition, at least part of what he means is that they are forms of apprehending what is singular or individual. To characterize space and time as forms of intuition is to characterize them in terms of a certain function that they play in the way in which we relate to the world; i.e., it is to characterize them in terms of the place they have in our cognitive connection to our experience. Our notion of an individual is ultimately inseparable from the fact that our ontology is spatio-temporal. By the ideality of space and time Kant means something stronger than this fact that space and time have a central role in our cognitive connection to experience. He means to imply that space and time make no sense apart from or are to be analyzed only in terms of this function. It is not as if space and time are basic features of the world itself and that they (also) have a central function in our connection to the world, but rather that space and time are nothing apart from this function.

In order for space and time to be forms of intuition, they must in some sense be prior to what occupies them. We saw above (pp.

12–13) that the numerical differentiability of objects is secondary to the numerical differentiability of parts of space and time. It was because of this that Kant rejected any view of space and time as relations between already well-defined individuals. If space and time are to be prior in our thought to the individuality (numerical differentiability) of objects, then they must be absolute, not relational. But for Kant absolute space and time considered as objective would be two *Undinge*. What Kant is saying is that somehow it does not make sense to suppose that space and time are features of the world itself; that considered as such they are mere *Undinge*.

Trendelnburg insisted that Kant overlooked a certain possibility in his discussion in the Aesthetic; namely, that space and time are elements of the world itself as well as being forms of our intuition (Vaihinger, 1881–82, 2: 135–36). Kant does not overlook this possibility; he rejects it. He does not say that we can never know whether things in themselves are spatial and temporal, that for all we know they might be; rather, he asserts quite definitely that they are not. Thus he says ". . . time is only a condition of appearances, not of things in themselves" (CPR, A 539, B 568, p. 468). Or, "This inner appearance cannot be admitted to exist in any such manner in and by itself; for it is conditioned by time, and time cannot be a determination of a thing in itself" (CPR, A 492, B 521, p. 440). Or again, "The non-sensible cause of these representations is completely unknown to us, and cannot therefore be intuited by us as object. For such an object would have to be represented as neither in space nor in time (these being merely conditions of sensible representation) . . . " (CPR, A 494, B 522, p. 441). Note that in this last passage Kant says both that things in themselves are completely unknowable and yet that they are definitely neither spatial nor temporal. This only makes sense if Kant thinks that space and time, by their very nature, could not apply to things in themselves. In other words, to correctly understand what space and time are and what is meant by things in themselves is ipso facto, according to Kant, to understand that things in themselves are not in space and time.

This last remark suggests one direction in which we can go in giving a first vague interpretation of transcendental idealism. If space and time are *Undinge* when considered apart from their function in our cognitive connection to experience as forms of intuition, then it would be plausible to say that things in themselves could *not* be spatial or temporal, if we understood by things in themselves, things considered apart from our cognitive connection to experience. Space and time do not apply to the world in itself, but only to the world in terms of our cognitive connection to our experience. The idea that certain notions apply not to the world itself but to our cognitive relation to experience is best understood in reference to the categories. What I am claiming in advance is that the point that things in themselves are not in space and time is to be understood on the same model as the claim, say, that things in themselves are not in causal connection. What this model is has, of course, not yet been made precise.

Kant says in the First Analogy, "This permanence is however, simply the mode in which we represent to ourselves the existence of things in the [field of] appearance" (CPR, A 168, B 229, p. 216). The concept of substance is a concept of things as represented by us. Part of the force of saying this is that a simple correspondence relation cannot be set up between our use of the concept of substance on the one hand and features of the world on the other. Involved in the very concept of substance is that it is a way of organizing our experience. For Kant, organization is not to be found in the world itself, at least not that type of organization implied in the categories. To say that the world is organized under the concept of substance is not to say that the world is itself so organized as to enable us to judge under the subject-predicate form of judgment, for judging under this form constitutes part of that organization. To say that the world is organized in terms of causality is not to say, e.g., that there are constant conjunctions in the world. Necessity is involved in the concept of causality (or in causal organization), and this necessity is to be analyzed in terms of the kinds of judgments we make and the use we make of them (in terms of the fact that we judge counterfactually to determine time-position). In other words, part of the organization involved in a category refers to the fact that we judge of the world under certain forms.

The categories are analyzed *functionally* by Kant. The meaning of the categories derives from the part they play in enabling us to get along with a spatio-temporal ontology. Part of the notion of substance, e.g., makes reference to its function of enabling us to handle judgments such as x came to be P at time t at place p (see section 9, above). It is not that we apply the concept of substance *and* that it serves this function, but rather that serving this function is part of what is meant by the concept. Similarly, part of what is meant by the concept of causality is that it serves as a rule for inferring formal from real relations (see section 12, above). Take away this function and we are left either with Hume's constant conjunction or with the mere form of a hypothetical judgment, neither of which are sufficient for the notion of causal connection. Making certain sorts of statements are basic to having a spatio-temporal ontology (statements to the effect that x came to be at some time at some place, that x preceded y or occurred at the same time as y, etc.). The connection of the relational categories to the possibility of making such kinds of statements form part of what is meant by having and applying such categories.

Let us return to the question of the *functional* interpretation of space and time that makes them, like the categories, aspects of the world not in itself but only in terms of our cognitive connection to experience. Spatiality and temporality are not (originally) general concepts that apply to a plurality of objects. If I say that x is red I do not thereby preclude that y or z are also red, whereas if I say that x is at p at t, I do thereby preclude that y or z ($\neq$ x) are at p at t. This "fact" is not to be understood as a feature of the world itself. It is rather a statement of what it is to have a spatio-temporal ontology. It is a statement to the effect that to have a spatio-temporal ontology is to delimit what constitutes individual objects on the basis ultimately of spatio-temporal location.

But is it not a feature of the world itself that two objects cannot be in the same place at the same time? Suppose we worked with an abstract ontology and talked, say, in terms of blueness being instantiated here and now, squareness being instantiated here and now, and so on. In this ontology the objects are universals, and it is certainly possible for a plurality of such "objects" to be instantiated at the same place at the same time. This ontology is quite compatible with the fact that we experience spatially and temporally (in the sense that certain of the sense qualities of our experience are spatial in nature), for some abstract universals like squareness would only be employed in experience by a subject whose sense qualities included those of the spatial variety. Though this ontology is compatible with a spatial experience in this way, it is not therefore a spatio-temporal ontology. Spatiality and temporality are not only features of our experience (sense features) but are such as to dominate the way in which we judge of (relate to) this experience. We shall disregard the question of why an abstract ontology is not feasible. The present point is merely that not any way of relating to the world in terms involving space and time (squareness, etc.) is ipso facto relating to it in terms of a spatio-temporal ontology. Also involved is the understanding of the *primary* function or role that space and time play in the notion of an object (a role so central that we speak of a *spatio-temporal* ontology).

Space and time must be viewed in their relation to the identity and individuality of what is given in them. To understand space and time is to understand that they are not general sharable predicates of what "inhabits" them and to understand this is not to understand something about the world in itself, but rather something about the role space and time play in an ontology if it is to be a spatio-temporal ontology.

We have indicated that part of the very understanding of substance, causality, space, and time involves a reference to how they function in our cognitive relation to our experience, where this latter relation involves primarily having and working with an (spatio-temporal) ontology. Having a certain ontology is itself not something derived from the world; rather it is something contributed to experience. To have an ontology is to think of or relate to experience as consisting of objects. The notion of an object is itself, for Kant, a notion that makes sense only vis-à-vis judgment. Being composed of objects does not describe a feature of how the world is in itself; it is a description of the world only in relation to a judging subject. The primary notion of an object is that which is judged. Judgment introduces the distinction between what is being talked about versus that which is being said about it, and it is this distinction that forms the core of the notion of an object as that which is judged or that to which reference is (purportedly) made. The point is that the very concept of an object only makes sense if we bring in the notion of judgment or the idea of how we intellectually relate to the world, and in this respect the notion of an object is not descriptive of anything in the world itself (apart from this relation). This is just to say that to have an ontology in Kant's sense is to have a semantics; it is to have a way of relating judgment to experience.*

To see this is also to see that in the most important sense there is

---

* That connection between a judging subject and his experience that is summed up in saying that he can judge of what he experiences I call the *cognitive* connection between the subject and his experience. That structure that his judgments must have if the cognitive relation is to be possible I call the *semantic* structure. That unity introduced into his experience by the structure of his judgments I term the epistemic unity of what is experienced.

no significance in saying that an ontology is faithful to or true to the world, is a copy of how the world is, or conforms to the way things are. The conforming relation is a relation between judgments and objects, not one between judgment and a de-ontologized experience. Whether a judgment is true or not obviously depends on what is being referred to by the judgment (or, more strictly, what is being referred to by that aspect of the judgment whose function is reference, i.e., the subject term). Unless we know what we (at least purport to) refer to, all questions of conformity are senseless. But a de-ontologized experience is precisely one that is not hooked up to the referring aspect of judgments. To ask whether an ontology is true to experience is to ask whether a system (generally) delineating purported reference is true to experience. But this is to introduce the question of "conformity to" or "being true to" prior to the establishment of the terms between which the conformity relation holds.

There being no sense to the question of the conformity of an ontology to the way things are is made less objectionable by the point that an ontology "leaves everything open." An ontology sets up the possibility of judgment without delimiting which judgments are true, for it sets up the semantics according to which it is possible to make false (purportedly true) judgments as well as true ones. Kant says, ". . . these rules of the understanding are not only true a priori, but are indeed the source of all truth (that is, of the agreement of our knowledge with objects) . . ." (CPR, A 237, B 296, p. 258). How rules that are the source of all truth can themselves be true a priori is not quite obvious. It suffices to say for the moment that an ontology can be true to the cognitive character of the subject, not to the sensible manifold constituting his experience.

I have been suggesting that the categories and space and time are comprehensible only via reference to their function in a spatio-temporal ontology, and that an ontology is not a feature of what is experienced, but is to be characterized only by reference to how a subject relates (intellectually) to what is experienced. To say that an ontology is something contributed by the subject is to say that the very notion of an object makes essential reference to (the judgmental apparatus of) the subject, that apart from reference to this apparatus the notion of an object collapses or is empty. It is important for Kant's purposes that this idea that certain notions relate primarily to our getting along with our experience, rather than to the world itself, make sense independently of there being equally viable alternative ways of getting along since for Kant there is but one viable ontology (for subjects with our cognitive structure). The course of my remarks has been directed to making some preliminary sense of this idea.

a) *Included in the analysis of certain concepts (space, time, causality, substance) is the function they play in our having a spatio-temporal ontology.* This is true irrespective of the possibility of alternative concepts having these functions. For example, the notion of substance was defined as a way of organizing states of affairs that enables us to distinguish their coming to be from their continuing to be (see section 9, above). In this respect, substance is a concept making reference not to the world itself but rather in terms of our relating to experience by having and working with a spatio-temporal ontology. It remains such a concept even if the organization implied is the only one enabling us to make these distinctions.

b) *Having an ontology is itself analyzed in terms of how we relate semantically to experience.* The world being composed of objects is another way of saying that what is experienced is related to our judgmental apparatus of referring and predicating. An object is that which has properties, that of which we are conscious as distinct from us (see pp. 43–44, above), and that of which we judge. All these characterizations are, for Kant, different ways of saying the same thing. That which has properties is that which is referred to in order to go on to predicate upon it. We distinguish ourselves from what is given to us by making what is given to us an object of judgment (see pp. 43–44, above). An ontology thus refers to the way subjects relate to the world (and so we speak of *our having* an ontology rather than the world having an ontology). To understand the notion of an object (as primarily an object of judgment) is to understand that it makes reference to how a subject gets along intellectually with his experience. This remains true irrespective of there being alternative ways of getting along. Kant's position in this regard is perhaps ambiguous. He does talk of forms of sensible intuition other than our forms of space and time and even of an intellectual intuition; i.e., he talks of alternative kinds (though certainly not equally viable alternatives) of getting along. Part of the motive for this kind of talk is certainly to enable us to understand that having an ontology refers primarily to how we relate to the world rather than to the world itself. Apart from this, however, there is to be found in the Transcendental Deduction an analysis of the notion of an object (as essentially an epistemic notion) that in itself suffices to establish the point that an ontology cannot be a feature of the world itself, but must bring in reference to how a subject's experience is connected to his judgmental apparatus.

20. *Contributions of the Subject*

Our preliminary discussion then has suggested the following: Certain basic aspects of our ordinary experience are contributed by the subject in the sense that these are essentially aspects of how the subject relates intellectually to his experience. They are "contributed by," "due to," or "derived from" the subject in the respect that they have *significance* only in reference to the subject, only in relation to how the subject intellectually connects to his experience.

Kant remarks, "the understanding is itself the source of nature, and so of its formal unity" (CPR, A 127, p. 148). Again, "the order and regularity in the appearances which we entitle *nature*, we ourselves introduce" (CPR, A 126, p. 147; see also A 159, B 198, pp. 194–95). We have already seen that the synthetic unity introduced by the categories is that whereby what is given in experience is interpreted under certain forms (see section 5, above). What Kant has in mind then is the kind of unity that experience can attain only by the introduction of an ontology. The organization of appearances at issue is their *intellectual* organization; i.e., their organization according to (in relation to) judgment forms. To judge under the subject-predicate form is to unify appearances in a certain way. To "objectify" appearances is to establish a connection (an epistemic connection) between experience and judgment (i.e., it is to make appearances objects of judgments). In other words, the formal unity of appearances that Kant is referring to is their epistemic unity. What is meant by we ourselves introducing this unity is that the concept of this unity essentially makes reference to us, to our judgmental apparatus. It does not make sense to say that the unity is to be found in the world itself (or in experience) for the unity consists precisely in the necessary relation of experience to our understanding (our forms of judgment). The understanding introduces this unity into experience in the sense that it is one of the *components* in terms of which this unity *is defined*. What we contribute to is the very definition or *concept* of this unity in the sense, say, that "water" contributes to the concept of being soluble in water. The judgmental apparatus of the subject forms part of the analysis of what this formal unity consists (it forms part of the concept of this unity). This unity does not make sense in abstraction from the judgmental apparatus of the subject any more than the notion of being soluble in water makes sense in abstraction from the notion of water. For the unity at issue here is an intellectual or epistemic one defined in terms of the relation of what is experienced to judgment, and so we cannot talk of this unity as deriving from the world itself (in abstraction from our judgment forms).

When Kant says that an organization of experience into objects is relative to us or is "to be met with only in ourselves" (CPR, A 130, p. 150), what he is saying is that the *notion* of an object depends on (includes in its analysis) reference to the judgmental apparatus of a subject. He is making a point about the dependence of the *concept* of an object on the *notion* of a (judging) subject, not any point about the dependence of the existence of objects upon the existence of subjects. Whether or not a substance is soluble in water does not depend on the existence of anything having the structure that makes up the physicist's concept of water. Similarly, whether the world is composed of objects does not depend on whether any subjects having or employing a judgmental apparatus exist. The notion of an object is relative to the *notion* of a judgmental apparatus (cognitive structure), but it is not relative to the existence of any subject employing that apparatus (or having that structure), just as the notion of being soluble in water is relative to the notion of water (as a certain structure type) but not to the existence of any water (of anything having that structure).

Kant makes a sharp distinction between association and affinity. Association is the accidental, nonintelligent collocation of appearances by way of suggestion or by way of a subjective propensity of the imagination to unite various elements in experience. Hume tried to trace the origin of certain complex concepts to such propensities to associate. In this way, e.g., he tried to "sensualize" the concept of an object; i.e., he tried to recreate how something might "look" to be an object, not indeed to the senses alone, but to the senses accompanied by the imagination's propensities to associate. Hume was interested in hooking up concepts to experience by finding the pictorial origin of the concept in experience. For Kant, the primary use the understanding makes of concepts is to judge by means of them. To apply a concept is to judge and so requires that appearances

already be established as "objective" (i.e., as objects of judgment).
It is this epistemic (formal) connection that Kant terms "affinity."
He refers to it as an "objective ground of all association of appearances" (CPR, A 122, p. 145). Establishing appearances as objective
does not consist in picturing them in a certain way, but rather in
judging according to semantic rules that connect judgment to its
object. Association is an organization of appearances based on
sensed similarities. Affinity, on the other hand, is an intellectual
organization.* Affinity is the ground of association in the sense that
it is the basis of any intellectual significance association can have.
The intellectual significance of association is as a basis for forming
specific empirical concepts. This in turn requires the general epistemic connection between experience and judgment

Affinity both conditions and is introduced by the unity of apperception. Kant, at times, identifies the unity of apperception with the
understanding. Thus, he says, "The unity of apperception in relation
to the synthesis of imagination is the understanding . . ." (CPR, A
119, p. 143), and again, "Indeed this faculty of apperception is the
understanding itself" (CPR, B 134n., p. 154). The unity of apperception would then be the unity of judgment since the understanding
is the faculty of judgment. Second, the unity of apperception is also
characterized as the unity of self-consciousness. For Kant, self-consciousness is the consciousness of a judging being, and so the unity
of apperception would then be the unity of consciousness of a judging being. Now part of what is involved in the unity of consciousness of such a being is the unity of his judgmental apparatus. A
necessary condition of someone's being one judging subject (consciousness) or one intelligence is that his judgments derive significance in terms of a single system of rules that connect judgment with
its object. Part of what it is for me to be the same intelligence now
as I was before is that my judgments "mean" the same now as before.
Thus, if I now judge that yesterday I saw a sunset, what is required
for the unity of myself as a judging consciousness is that the judgment 'I saw a sunset' has the same meaning as asserted by me now,
as it would have had, had I asserted it yesterday when I, indeed, saw
it. In saying that yesterday I (a self-conscious being) saw a sunset,
part of what I am now saying is that yesterday I could have correctly

---

* "It is this apperception that must be added to pure imagination in order to
render its function intellectual" (see CPR, A 124, p. 146).

made the judgment 'I see a sunset'. That I can *now* judge of what I saw yesterday is not enough for the ascription of self-consciousness to my (past) self. What is required is that I could have *then* judged of what I saw,* and if I am to be the *same* intelligence now as I was before I must be able to connect my present judgment to the effect that I saw a sunset yesterday with the judgment that could *then* have been made to the effect that I see a sunset. To have access to my past self as a judging (self-conscious) being or intelligence requires having access to the import or meaning of judgments I could (in the past) have made. But the import of a judgment is constituted at least in part by the semantical system that establishes the connection between judgment and its object and so the continuity of my (judging) consciousness involves the uniformity in the semantical system I employ. Thus, Kant can characterize the unity of apperception both as the unity of self-consciousness and the unity of understanding because the unity of a judging being involves the uniformity or unity in the import of the judgments he makes. The transition from the former to the latter characterization goes, then, as follows:

a) A self-conscious being is a judging being.

b) The unity of a judging being involves his having access to his past self as a judging being.

c) This, in turn, involves his being the same intelligence; i.e., his judgments having a uniform import or significance.

d) This, in turn, involves his judgments being made in accordance with a uniform system establishing the import of judgments.

e) And this latter is just the unity of the understanding as a faculty.

Now *affinity* is the intellectual (epistemic) unity of what is given in experience vis-à-vis *judgment*. Affinity refers, for example, to such "facts" of organization of what is given as that appearances are objects with properties. To say there is a thoroughgoing affinity of the manifold of experience is to say that all that is given in experi-

---

* Just as for me to judge of an animal that it sees a sunset is not sufficient for the ascription of intelligence or self-consciousness to the animal, for I must judge that he *could* make the judgment to the effect that (with the import of it being) he sees it.

ence can be connected to our forms of judgment, or that all that is given is amenable to our judgmental system. It follows from this that only if appearances are subject to this affinity can they be brought to the unity of self-consciousness, for only insofar as what is given is connected to my judgmental apparatus is it possible for me to judge of what is given and, further, only insofar as *all* that is given is connected to a uniform system of judgment is it possible for me to be the same intelligence from judgment to judgment, and so for me to be the identical subject of all that is given in experience.

Kant says,

> For the mind could never think its identity [as intelligence] in the manifoldness of its representations . . . if it did not have before its eyes the identity of its act [i.e., the uniformity in significance of the judgments it makes] whereby it subordinates all synthesis of apprehension (which is empirical) to a transcendental unity [i.e., the uniformity in the import of our judgments both requires and introduces an affinity in appearances, namely that they are one and all connected according to our judgmental system] hereby rendering possible their interconnection according to a priori rules (CPR, A 108, p. 137).

He says later on,

> According to this principle [the unity of apperception] all appearances without exception must so enter the mind or be apprehended that they conform to the unity of apperception. Without synthetic unity [affinity] in their connection this would be impossible; and such synthetic unity is itself therefore objectively necessary (CPR, A 122, p. 145).

In other words, unless all that is given was compatible with a uniform system establishing the import of our judgments (unless all appearances were subject to affinity in their connection) we could not maintain our identity as judging beings vis-à-vis all that is given (appearances would not conform to the unity of apperception). Thus, the affinity of appearances is required for the unity of apperception.

But what is it for appearances to be in thoroughgoing affinity?

It is nothing more than their being subject to the uniform system establishing the import of judgments. The affinity is not some sort of organization specifiable independent of our judgmental system. To say that all appearances are subject to affinity (synthetic unity) in their connection is to say, for example, that all appearances are objects having properties. But this, in turn, is just to say that all appearances are judged of in accordance with semantical rules of reference and predication. It is our judgmental system that "introduces" the affinity (in terms of which the affinity is characterized). In this respect, the affinity of appearances is constituted by the fact that we (as judging beings) are in connection with what is given in experience, and thus it is that the unity of apperception *introduces* the affinity. Kant says,

> This concept [of a transcendental object] cannot contain any determinate intuition and therefore refers only to that unity which must be met with in any manifold of knowledge which stands in relation to an object [i.e., in any judging form of consciousness]. This relation is nothing but the necessary unity of consciousness . . . (CPR, A 109, p. 137).

In other words, the affinity of all appearances (their organization as objects) is nothing more than the relation of all that is given in experience to our judgmental system, which itself is but an aspect of the unity of a judging consciousness with respect to all that is given.

It is, thus, the unity of our judgmental system, or the unity of our faculty of understanding (the one characterization of the unity of apperception) that both 1) introduces affinity into appearances and 2) forms an essential component (condition) of the unity of consciousness of a judging being (the other characterization of the unity of apperception), for 1) to say that all appearances are subject to affinity in their connection is to say that all that is given in experience is connected in terms of our uniform system of judgment and 2) it is only because our judgmental connection to appearances is uniform that we maintain our intellectual identity (our identity as judging beings) through experience. Both the unity of a judging subject and the unity for judgment of what is given to him in experience derive from the uniformity of the semantic system in terms of which his judgments have import or connection with what is given in experience.

The connection between formal unity (affinity) and sensible similarity (association) is important in understanding one aspect of Kant's empirical realism. A more detailed understanding of this doctrine must await the investigation of the notion of a thing in itself. For now, the important point is that affinity grounds (any cognitive significance of) association; it does not delimit it. Kant says, "Certainly, empirical laws, as such, can never derive their origin from pure understanding. This is as little possible as to understand completely the inexhaustible multiplicity of appearances merely by reference to the pure form of sensible intuition" (CPR, A 127, p. 148). In contributing certain elements to experience, the subject does not thereby distort in any way what is given through experience. This refers back to the remark above that our semantic connection to the world "leaves everything open." For example, the necessity aspect of causal connections is introduced by the subject insofar as this necessity consists in his taking features of appearances as licensing inferences to temporal relations. This, however, does not decide what in fact causes what; no empirical question as to which features are to be used in this way is thereby decided. What is introduced is the possibility of deciding (empirically) *whether or not* x is the *cause* of y (as opposed to the decision between whether x does or does not merely happen to precede y in experience). What is introduced is the significance of, or a way of taking (using), what experience gives.

On a more difficult level, let us consider the subject contributing space and time to experience. We must keep in mind a distinction between what is given in experience as including spatial and temporal characteristics versus what is given in experience being in space and in time. For example, a subject experiences spatially if what is given to him has shape and size, even if this mere experience of them is limited to their purely qualitative aspect. He experiences temporally if he has what might be called qualitative "feelings" of duration or precedence. What is given being in space and in time, however, refers primarily not to its qualitative (or even quantitative) characteristic, but rather to its localizability along with (vis-à-vis) whatever else is given in experience. This thoroughgoing localizability is a presumption of making *either* the judgment that x preceded y or the judgment that y preceded x. Both of these judgments are made regarding x's and y's position in that time wherein whatever is given through experience must have location vis-à-vis all else that is given. The decision between the two judgments is an empirical matter (is left open to experience), though their common presumption, the unity of space and time (and the implied thoroughgoing localizability), is a contribution of the subject. (For what the unity of space and time consists in is to be understood in reference to their function as forms of individuation.)

Speaking of the "order and regularity" in appearances, Kant says, "We could never find them in appearances, had not we ourselves or the nature of our mind originally set them there (CPR, A 129, p. 147). We could never find in (judge on the basis of) experience that x preceded y or that x caused y, or even that x is red unless we already related to the world in terms of a spatio-temporal ontology. But nevertheless it is on the basis of experience that any empirical judgment is made, and it is this fact that constitutes one aspect of Kant's empirical realism. Kant sometimes calls his idealism a *formal* idealism and his realism a *material* (contentual) realism. Our material relation to the world is a realistic one in the sense that the content of a judgment must be based on or conform to our experience. The distinction between form and content and its relevance to transcendental idealism requires an understanding of the notion of a thing in itself to which we now turn.

21. The Notion of A Thing in Itself

There could be no justification of synthetic a priori knowledge, no objective reality of the categories, no experience, no empirical knowledge, if what we had to deal with were things in themselves. The subject could not introduce unity into experience if that experience was of things in themselves. This notion of a thing in itself is a central notion of the doctrine of transcendental idealism. It is also, however, the most difficult notion in Kant's philosophy. For that reason I have delayed its discussion until we have gained some insight regarding that aspect of transcendental idealism expressed in such phrases as the subject contributes or introduces certain elements into experience, or certain aspects of the world are due to or derive from the structure of the subject, and so on.

One characterization of the idea of a thing in itself is as a limiting concept, and it is usually interpreted as limiting the domain of human access; i.e., it is taken as a kind of thing that if it (they) existed we could have no *knowledge* either that it (they) did or what properties it (they) had. According to this line of interpretation, when Kant makes remarks to the effect that the categories do not apply to things in themselves, his point may be that we cannot *know* any concept at all (and so a fortiori the categories) applies to objects beyond our access. In other words the notion of a thing in itself serves a limiting function by reminding us that there may be more things in heaven and earth than are dreamt of in the Transcendental Deduction. We are simply being called on to be forever modest in the reach of our knowledge.

There is, however, a more significant strain of thought that runs through Kant's remarks about things in themselves. It is not the notion of a kind of object inexorably unknown to us, but rather the notion of a *concept* quite literally incomprehensible to us. This idea of incomprehensibility should alert us to the fact that "thing in itself" refers to a different *concept* of an object than our concept of an object. We have argued that a central tenet of the Metaphysical and Transcendental Deductions is that the notion of an object is the epistemic one of an object of judgment (see p. 43, above); that to say the world is composed of objects and to say that experience is epistemically connected to judgment forms is to say the same thing twice over. It this way the *very notion* of an object brings in reference to the judgmental apparatus of the subject. What I propose is that the notion of a thing in itself be interpreted as the notion of a non-epistemic *concept* of what it is to be an *object*. It is an alternative conception of what is involved in being an object; the idea, namely, of a concept of an object that would have sense apart from any reference to how the experience of a subject hooks up epistemically to his intellectual (judgmental) structure. Again, the notion of a thing in itself is that concept of an object according to which being an object or a thing would make sense in abstraction from any idea of a (type of) subject and his intellectual organization of his experience.

According to the epistemic notion of an object, nothing could be an object *in itself* (apart from bringing in the idea of a subject), simply because according to this concept what it is for something to be an object involves reference to how a subject relates semantically to his experience. The notion of something being a thing in itself, on the other hand, is just that *notion* of an object that does not require for the completion of its sense any reference at all to so much as the idea of a subject. It seems to me that we are here at the center of Kant's Copernican Revolution. His point is that to ask the question "What is an object?" can only be to ask the question "How does the experience of some subject connect up to his judgmental apparatus?" It is in this regard that the *notion* of a judging subject becomes the central one in Kant's philosophy.

It is important to understand how *little* the notions of what we have access to, or what is knowable to us, is the basic one in this interpretation of a thing in itself. Kant mentions the possibility of forms of intuition other than space and time. It is clear that for Kant we can have no access to what is not in space and time, yet he does not think the objects of such an alternative sensible intuition are, in any respect, things in themselves. For example, he thinks the categories would apply for a subject with such a type of intuition *in a sense quite analogous* to the way in which they apply in our experience. He would not make such a claim about the relation of categories to things in themselves. In talking of things in themselves Kant is not making the point that we need experience in order to know an object, that "concepts without intuitions are empty," and a thing in itself, being a non-sensible object is thus beyond access. It is not primarily that experience is required to gain access to objects; it is the stronger claim that the very notion of an object is essentially the notion of how what is given to a subject independently of his judgment is connected epistemically to the subject's faculty of understanding. *It is not that experience is required for the* knowledge *of objects, but rather experience is one term of the cognitive relation in terms of which the very notion of an object is to be understood.*

As Kant employs the notion of the given, it is one of the correlates between which the cognitive relation is supposed to be established. The given is that to which the understanding with its judgment forms must connect; it is always given to the understanding "from elsewhere." It is because experience (or more technically, the given) is required as being that to which judgment has to connect that our very notion of an object (itself an epistemic notion, "object of judgment") is tied down to the *notion* of experience (the given). The primary importance of experience for knowledge is not that the former is required in order that we can have *access* to things, but rather the following: knowledge, for Kant, is always knowledge of objects; this in the sense that knowledge is judgmental (and "object" means "object of judgment"). We have knowledge when how we *think* the way things are conforms to the way they are. In other words, knowledge is a matter of our judgments conforming to what they are judgments of. In this respect knowledge presupposes for its sense (not its attainment) the establishment of a connection between what we are supposed to have (or try to get) knowledge of with judgment. It is at this point that the *notion* of experience, of something being given to which judgment is to connect (i.e., as something serving as the correlate to judgment) becomes important for the possibility of the sense or significance of knowledge.

Kant's discussion of the positive and negative senses of noumenon can, I think, be understood in terms of our interpretation of the notion of a thing in itself. He says we try to form for ourselves a positive conception of a noumenon by introducing the notion of an intellectual intuition or an intuitive understanding (CPR, B 308, pp. 269–70). Kant, of course, decries this as illicit, but it is as important to understand why this would be the way to try (albeit abortively) to form a positive conception of a thing in itself as it is to understand why it is illicit. On our interpretation the notion of a thing in itself is the notion of a concept of an object that does not require for its sense any reference to a cognitive subject. This is opposed to our notion of an object (thing) that has for its content or meaning the semantic connection of a subject with what is given to him. Now, introducing an intellectual intuition is bringing in reference to a type of cognitive subject; i.e. it is trying to understand the notion of a thing in itself on the model of our epistemic conception of an object. It is quite clear why we must fail in this way to form a positive conception of a thing in itself. This latter notion cannot be understood on the model of our conception of an object, for it is precisely our conception with which it is meant to be contrasted. It is also, however, clear why this would be the way to attempt to form a positive conception of a thing in itself, for the only positive (meaningful) conception we have of an object is our epistemic conception. We do not know what other content could be given to the concept of an object. We do not know what else could be meant by the notion of an object (other than, of course, merely negating what the content of our conception of an object is).

We have argued that a thing in itself is not a different kind of thing, nor even a concept of a different kind of thing, but rather a different kind of concept of a thing. We have now to consider what limiting function such a concept might play, since we have urged that this limiting is not primarily the limiting of what we can know to what we can have access to by way of experience. The concept of a thing in itself is employed by Kant to limit the scope of a priori knowledge (the categories and space and time). This limitation can be interpreted in two ways. First, it has often been taken by commentators as a limitation of the *domain* of objects to which the categories apply. This limitation is merely a corollary of Kant's repeated assertions to the effect that "concepts without intuitions are empty." We cannot apply any concepts at all (and a fortiori we cannot apply the categories) to things in themselves because things in themselves are the kinds of objects in relation to which we would have no intuitions corresponding to our concepts. There is, however, a different way in which the notion of a thing in itself limits a priori knowledge; a way that is, I think, more basic to Kant's transcendental idealism.

The notion of a thing in itself serves not so much to mark off the domain *of objects* of which we can have knowledge, but rather to mark off the domain (part) *of our knowledge* that can be a priori. The important connection is that the subject could not contribute or introduce elements if what he had to deal with were things in themselves. We have argued that the subject contributes or introduces a certain unity just in the sense that the very conception of this unity makes essential reference back to the subject; i.e., it is the *concept* of a subject that contributes to or is part of the concept of this (epistemic) unity. Implicit in this is a principle that I think is central to Kant's transcendental idealism in a number of ways; the principle, namely, that this is the *only* sense in which we can justifiably speak of the subject contributing elements into his experience. Before considering the important implications of this principle, let us note that the limitation that the subject can contribute only in this way is what is expressed by the claim that the subject could contribute nothing if what he had to deal with was the concept of a thing in itself. The concept of a thing in itself is the idea of a concept of a thing or an object that would not require for its sense any reference back to a subject; it would not require the notion of a subject to complete its content. That the subject could not introduce anything with regard to things in themselves comes down to saying that reference to a subject may not form part of the concept of a thing, if the kind of concept of a thing we have in mind is a concept of a thing that does not have as part of its content any reference to a subject (i.e., if it is the concept of a thing in itself). The notion of a thing in itself thus expresses a limitation on what the subject can contribute in that it clarifies or defines in what sense the subject can be said to contribute elements to his experience (only as being part of the concept of these elements). We have still to discuss the consequences of this principle (namely, that the subject can only contribute elements that require for completion of their sense reference back to the subject himself) for Kant's transcendental or formal idealism.

22. *Transcendental Idealism and Empirical Realism*

The notion of a formal element is central to Kant's idealism, which, as we have seen, he even characterizes as a formal idealism. Being idealistic in certain aspects is noxious, while being idealistic in other aspects is not. The line for Kant is drawn by the transcendental-empirical or the formal-material distinction. The question is how is this line drawn. The nonnoxiousness of idealism revolves about the notions of distortion and arbitrariness. For Kant the subject contributes elements to experience in a nondistortive, yet nonarbitrary, way. An idealism with regard to the *formal* aspects of experience is nonnoxious in that it is nondistortive. We have seen that at least part of Kant's empirical realism is that everything is "left open" that *could* be left open. By "left open" here I mean undecidable on a priori grounds or not in any sense contributed by the subject; left open to experience. The question is what could and could not be left open. The edge of Kant's response is that those elements the very concepts of which essentially make reference to the fundamental ways in which a subject gets on cognitively with his experience cannot be left up to the discretion of experience. An element is fundamental if it is required to establish the realistic relation in the first place. The realistic relation is that in which experience is that to which conceptualization conforms rather than vice versa. Kant is saying that the presuppositions of the realistic relation cannot themselves be analyzed on the model of this relation. The fundamentality here is in relation to the subject's *cognitive* connection to the world; i.e., Kant is not talking of the most fundamental (pervasive) facts about the world (force, gravitation, etc.).

For Kant, a formal aspect of experience is an organizational or combinatorial aspect. The type of organization implied is an *intellectual* or significatory organization. If we recall that the subject contributing an element is to be interpreted as the *notion* of a subject being a part of the *concept* of the element, then it makes sense as a general principle that formal elements are contributed by the subject. Intellectual organization is precisely that type of organization that includes reference to the notion of a cognitive subject. We have interpreted this organization or unity as an epistemic one, which is just to say that this unity, in its concept, makes essential reference to the notion of a judging subject. The primary unpacking of the notion of a *formal* element is thus that of an element that consists in experience being organized in a certain cognitive way. It is not that experience must in itself have a certain unity if, say, judgment is to be possible, but more radically judgment introduces this unity (in the sense that what this unity consists of can only be defined in reference to judgment; it is an epistemic unity).

Even the contribution of space and time as forms of intuition ought, I think, to be analyzed along these lines. The unity or singleness of space or time comes down to (or is to be understood in terms of) their cognitive function as forms of individuation. It is true that for Kant this function is attributed to intuition "prior to" conceptualization, and we have followed Kant in this regard (see section 1, above). What I am claiming, however, is that this function of space and time as forms of individuation is nevertheless an incipient cognitive function. Sheer manifoldness, which space and time make possible, is an intuitive matter, but recognizing a manifold as a manifold is not. Ultimately, space and time as forms of individuation deriving from their singleness have no completed sense until their function in relation to our judgment about experience is brought in. The unity of space and time are not to be understood as the unity of two *things,* but rather in terms of the role space and time play in setting up an (spatio-temporal) ontology.*

The relevance of this notion of formality to the nonnoxiousness of transcendental idealism is as follows. Suppose x is some condition such that unless x held or obtained experience would be impossible or our connection to experience would be impossible. If this were the only basis for saying that therefore the subject contributes x (as if x were too important to be left up to the world) transcendental

---

* The problem is how to make the *intuitive* nature of space and time compatible with their being *cognitive* notions of how we relate *intelligently (intellectually)* with experience. See the tortuous n. a to B 160, pp. 170–71.

idealism would be a sham, open, for example, to the kinds of objections that Stroud brings forth (1968, pp. 254–57). The necessity (indispensability) of x's obtaining still leaves open the question whether x does in fact obtain or not. For example, in Kant's ethics the notion of freedom is an indispensable postulate, but he is quite insistent that this does not establish the *objective reality* of freedom. Also, in the Dialectic Kant argues that certain regulative ideas are indispensable in making full use of the understanding, but this indispensability does not establish their objective reality.* Now it is evident that Kant does not think of the categories in this way, as merely indispensable postulates of theoretical thought (CPR, B 167–68, pp. 174–75). The rationale of this is that the basis for the subject contributing x is not merely or primarily x's indispensability, but rather x's formality; i.e., *its being not a feature of the world itself that we require in order to relate to the world but rather a feature that makes sense only in terms of (or is introduced by) that relation.* Take, for example, the very notion of an object. For Kant, it does not make sense to say that, although admittedly the world being composed of objects is indispensable to the possibility of our relating to the world, still it does not follow that the world itself really is composed of objects. The world itself being composed of objects is nonsense, for the world being composed of objects is just our relating to experience cognitively (judgmentally). It makes no sense to say that a *formal* element may not, after all, really obtain or be found in the world itself as if it ought to be, as if unless it were we would be dealing merely with our own chimeras. One cannot object that we ought not relate to the world as being composed of objects unless our so relating corresponds to the world itself really being composed of objects, or that we may relate to the world as composed of objects yet this may not be the way it really is, for our relating to the world cognitively is identical to its being composed of objects. There is no feature of the world itself that is the basis of our relating to it in a formal way; our relating to it in this way is precisely what it means for the world to have this feature. Kant says "We could never find them [order and regularity] in appearances had not we ourselves,

---

* See the appendix to the Dialectic. A transcendental deduction of the ideas is impossible (CPR, A 664, B 692, p. 546). The ideas are regulative, not constitutive (CPR, A 664, B 692, p. 546). They are (mere) *maxims* of reason (CPR, A 666, B 694, p. 547).

or the nature of our mind originally set them there" (CPR, A 125, p. 147).

We must conceptualize in terms of *causal* connections, but still are causal connections really to be found in the world? Does our conceptualization correspond to the world itself? To understand the formal nature of causality is to understand the nonsense of this question. The element of necessity that is involved in the notion of a *causal* connection is our use of the hypothetical judgment counterfactually in relation to time-determination. It makes no sense to ask whether this use corresponds to some necessity in the world defined apart from this use (though it does, of course, make sense to say that *which* judgments we make use of in this way depends on what is given in experience. Again, the introduction of causal necessity on the part of the subject sets up the possibility of making false *causal* judgments as well as true ones).

The nonnoxiousness of *formal* idealism, then, consists in two interconnected aspects:

> 1) It leaves everything about the world itself open that could be left open, for the subject contributes only those elements that it makes no sense to think of as elements of the world itself (e.g., the subject, in judging a certain way, introduces causal necessity; in judging, period, introduces objects, etc.)
>
> 2) It precludes the question of whether the world itself possesses those elements that the subject contributes and requires to get along in the world, again *for the exact same reason* that the subject contributes only those elements that it makes no sense to think of as elements of the world itself.*

We are now in a position, I think, to understand the connection in Kant's thought between transcendental idealism and empirical

---

* Kant says (CPR, B 163–64, p. 172), "The question therefore arises, how it can be conceivable that nature should proceed in accordance with the categories that yet are not derived from it, and do not model themselves upon its pattern.

"That the *Laws* of appearances in nature must agree with the understanding of its *a priori* form, that is, with its faculty of *combining* the manifold in general [is not surprising for] . . . the laws do not exist in the appearances, but only relatively to this same being insofar as it has understanding."

realism on the one hand and transcendental realism and empirical idealism on the other. The transcendental realist is working with the concept of a thing in itself. For the transcendental realist the notion of an object cannot involve as part of its sense any reference to a subject. He holds this position because an object is precisely that which is not up to the subject, that which is what it is regardless of how the subject thinks of it. But there is a confusion here on his part, for this latter point is true of objects only in an empirical sense; (only after the epistemic relation between the subject and his experience has been established for prior to this there is no sense to the notion of an object at all). The transcendental realist fallaciously concludes from the correct point that what any object is like is independent of how we think or judge of it, to the idea that the abstract notion of an object must make sense independently of any reference to our judgmental apparatus. We can give no content to this latter notion of an object. If we abstract from the cognitive relation between the subject and his experience we are left without any positive idea of an object. It is the transcendental realist who thus becomes the empirical idealist, in that for him what we know empirically are not objects because empirical knowledge gives us objects only in the epistemic sense, which, for him, is to say it does not give us objects at all.

Kant's point is that empirical judgment presupposes contributions on the part of the subject and that this does not destroy the notion of an object; on the contrary, it establishes the only positive conception of an object. The reference to the judgmental apparatus of the subject in the very notion of an object is not, for the transcendental idealist, incompatible with the idea that what an object is like does not depend on what the subject judges it or thinks it to be like. Recognizing this, and recognizing that we can have empirical knowledge (we can judge) of objects in this sense, he does not degrade what our empirical judgments are of to mere illusion as does the transcendental realist. In this way it is the transcendental idealist who, working with the correct conception of an object (not as thing in itself), can maintain an empirical realism. Kant is saying that certain basic aspects of our experience make sense only in reference to a subject (most startlingly, the very notion of an object), but, properly understood, the independence from the subject required for something to be an object (independence in the empirical sense that our judgments must conform to how things are) is not thereby contradicted.

The contribution of certain elements on the part of the subject interpreted transcendentally means that these elements in their very concept make reference to a subject. This is not to be confused with a subject contributing elements in an empirical sense that would mean the subject making things up (inventing things) rather than basing his judgments on experience. This latter would indeed be a noxious, distorting form of idealism. Kant is saying that it is the transcendental realist who first falls into "illusion" by distorting the very notion of an object. It is the transcendental realist who invents a merely negative, empty concept of an object that he then rejects as merely negative and empty.

It is along these lines that Kant's criticism of Berkeley in the following passage proceeds (although not necessarily the way Berkeley himself proceeds):

> For if we regard space and time as properties which, if they are to be possible at all, must be found in the things in themselves, and if we reflect on the absurdities in which we are then involved, in that two infinite things which are not substances, nor anything actually existing in substances, must yet have existence, nay, must be the necessary condition of the existence of all things . . . we cannot blame the good Berkeley for degrading bodies to mere illusion (CPR, B 70–71; p. 89; see also B 275, p. 244).

What Kant is saying is that Berkeley concluded from the (transcendental) ideality of space to the (empirical) ideality of what is in space. Berkeley, according to Kant, recognized that space and time could not be features of the world itself (that they make essential reference to the subject) and concluded that anything that required space and time for its existence could not be characterized as an object for it is conditioned by what requires reference to a subject, and, according to the notion of an object as a thing in itself, this is absurd. On the other hand, for Kant there are ways in which essential reference to a subject is not incompatible with the notion of an object (on the contrary, it gives content to the notion) and, in particular, the transcendental ideality of space and time are compatible with the empirical reality of what has space and time as a condition of its existence.

Summary

We may now review the interpretations offered of the theses we took as constituting transcendental idealism (see p. 136, above).

a) Certain elements of experience derive from or are contributed by the subject.

The interpretation of this thesis, along with *b,* below, forms the base of our interpretation of transcendental idealism. A subject contributes elements to experience just in the sense that the very notion of the element makes reference to the concept of a cognitive subject. In other words, the *concept* of a subject contributes to (forms part of) the very notion of the element. Relatedly, the subject is the source of unity in experience in the sense that the concept of the unity referred to again involves reference to a cognitive subject, for it is essentially an intellectual or epistemic unity and so depends for its sense on the notion of and activity (i.e., judging) of an intellectual subject.

b) The subject could contribute nothing if what he had to deal with were things in themselves.

The notion of a thing in itself is the notion of that kind of concept of an object that does not allow for its completion or positive sense, any reference to the notion of a cognitive subject. This conception of the notion of a thing in itself plus the interpretation of thesis *a* above absolutely preclude a subject contributing elements to things in themselves. Reference to a subject cannot form part of the concept of an object if the kind of concept of an object involved is that of a thing in itself, namely, an object that can have as no part of its sense any reference to the notion of a subject.

The main thrust of the Metaphysical and Transcendental Deductions is that the notion of an object is an epistemic notion, not a notion of a thing in itself. To say what is experienced are objects and to say what is experienced is connected to our forms of judgment is to say the same thing. Just as the notion of truth, say, cannot apply to judgments by themselves, but to judgments only in relation to their object (i.e., what they are judgments of), and this makes truth a semantic rather than a syntactic notion, so, inversely, the notion of an object cannot apply to what is experienced by itself, but to what is experienced only in relation to judgment, and this makes the notion of an object an epistemic rather than an empirical one.

c) The categories do not have application or validity with respect to things in themselves.
The categories themselves are concepts of our cognitive relation to experience; i.e., the categories can be understood, or have content, only in terms of the functions they play in setting up a cognitive relation between the subject and his experience. Their very sense depends in this way on reference to a subject and so on the epistemic notion of an object. Again, it is the subject who introduces causal necessity, say, into experience by his employment of a certain judgment form (the hypothetical) to fulfill a certain function (time-determination).

d) Transcendental idealism leads to empirical realism; transcendental realism implies empirical idealism.
The transcendental realist is working with the notion of a thing in itself. He concludes from the quite correct empirical point that what an object is (what properties it has) it is (has) independently of what we think it is (what properties we judge it to have), to the transcendental point that the abstract concept of an object must make sense independently of any reference to the judging of a subject and his (cognitive) relation to his experience. But this kind of concept of an object is quite empty. The transcendental realist, in severing the notion of an object from how a subject relates to his experience, thinks he still has a meaningful notion of an object and a meaningful (but insoluble) problem of how the subject relates to such objects, and so is led to hold to an empirical idealism. For the transcendental idealist, there is no sense in thinking we are left with any meaningful notion of an object that would give any significance to the question of how we would relate to such objects.

e) Space and time are not objective features of the world by itself; they are mere forms of intuition.
Space and time in their very notion make reference to a cognitive subject. They are notions that cannot be understood if we abstract from their function in our relation to experience. Not merely does

the unity or singleness of space and time (which is their essential aspect) condition individuality (or serve as forms of individuality), but this unity itself consists precisely in their serving as such conditions (with all the implications this has for our relating significantly to our experience); it is not to be understood as the unity or singleness of a thing. One would almost like to say that the notions of space and time (sharing, as they do, with the categories an essential reference to how a subject relates to his experience in order to complete their sense) are epistemic notions.* They ultimately make reference to judgment in that they are to be completely understood only in reference to the part they play in determining our ontology (i.e., how we relate judgmentally to experience).

I have read or heard somewhere (I do not recall the source) that all Kant did was to take the kinds of organization Hume had attributed to propensities of the (reproductive) imagination and attribute them instead to categories of the understanding. This remark, if meant to belittle the difference between Kant and Hume, rather unwittingly gets to the source of the difference. Behind this shift from the imagination to the understanding is Kant's conception of our relation to the world as a cognitive or intelligent one and so to be sought for in the understanding, as opposed to Hume's conception of it as a causal or mechanical relation and so to be sought for in the imagination. It is perhaps not very surprising that in removing, as Hume did, notions involving intellectual significance or cognitive import, the very notion of a subject is also thereby removed, for we are, after all, cognitive beings. What is, however, quite surprising is Kant's fundamentally revolutionary insight that in removing such notions, the very notion of an object or of a world just as surely falls away.

---

* Again, there is the problem that space and time are *intuitively* understood.

Appendix: Syntheticity

The *synthetic* character of the principle of the Second Analogy derives from the following consideration. The argument for the principle that every event has a cause proceeds not from an analysis of the concept of an event or even from an analysis of the concept of a temporal event, but rather from an investigation of the conditions of the determinability of an event as temporal (as having a position in time). Kant says, "If the reader will go back to our proof of the principle of causality—that everything which happens, that is, every event, presupposes a cause—he will observe that we were able to prove it only of objects of possible experience, *and even so, not from pure concepts,* but only as a principle of the possibility of experience [italics mine]" (CPR, B 289, p. 253). C. I. Lewis correctly understands this point when he says ". . . Kant believed he had established that being a temporal event *entails* being caused through the necessities of all possible experience and representation, but that this connection is not derivable from the *concepts* or *definitions* of 'temporal event' and 'cause' " (Lewis, 1946, p. 161). Lewis objects, however, ". . . anything which is essential to the temporal character of an event must be included in the adequate concept of it as a temporal event . . . A definition which does not entail logically all characters essential to what is defined, is faulty" (Lewis, 1946, pp. 161, 163). Lewis, thus, has the following standard of adequacy of definition: If P is essentially (a priori) connected to S, then P forms part of an adequate definition of S. This standard, of course, precludes any possibility of *synthetic* a priori judgments, for it states that if 'S is P' is a priori, then P is part of an adequate definition of S, and so P forms part of the subject concept 'S', and so 'S is P' is analytic.

Let us not dispute Lewis's standard of adequacy and instead make a distinction between two kinds of judgments:

1) *Analyticity*—'S is P' is *analytic* if the concept 'P' forms part of, or is included in, the concept 'S'.

2) *Recursive (strict) analyticity*—'S is P' is *recursively analytic* if

    a) 'S' is a *simple* concept and 'P' is the same concept as 'S'.

    b) 'S' is a *compound* concept with components, say, 'S$_1$', 'S$_2$', and either

        I) 'P' forms part of the concept 'S$_1$',

        II) 'P' forms part of the concept 'S$_2$',

        III) 'P' can be broken down into components 'P$_1$', . . . , 'P$_n$' such that each 'P$_i$' either forms part of the concept 'S$_1$' or part of the concept 'S$_2$'.

For example, *A*) 'A bachelor is unmarried' and *B*) 'A bald bachelor is an unmarried man without hair' are both recursively analytic; *A* by part b-I of the definition and *B* by part b-III. Both judgments are also, of course, analytic. On the other hand, *C*) 'A determinably temporal event is caused' is analytic if we accept Lewis's standard of adequacy, but it is not, it seems, *recursively* analytic. Whatever the difficulties in distinguishing simple from compound concepts, 'temporal event' surely is a compound concept. So *C* does not meet 2a. Nor does it seem that the concept of causality forms part of the concept 'temporal' (2bI) or part of the concept 'event' (2bII). Further, it is not at all apparent that 'cause' can be analyzed into components such that each component forms part of either the concept 'temporal' or the concept 'event' (2bIII).

All recursively analytic judgments are also, of course, analytic in the first sense. Let us make one more definition:

3) *Emergent analyticity*—'S is P' is *emergently analytic* if 'S is P' is analytic, but 'S is P' is not recursively analytic. What I wish to suggest is that the *use* Kant makes of the distinction between analytic and synthetic judgments can be accounted for if we take the distinction to be that between recursively analytic and emergent analytic judgments. It accounts for Kant's use of the distinction in that it correctly marks out the separation of a priori judgments into two classes, and it is serviceable as the tool Kant wants against the method of Leibnizian rationalism.

Mathematical judgments seem interpretable as emergently analytic. Take, for example, the judgment 'A four-sided equiangular figure has its diagonals equal'. The equality of the diagonals (P) follows from the four-sidedness *together* with the equiangularity, but P does not follow from either concept alone, nor is P analyzable into components each of which follows from one of the concepts alone. Similarly, the subject and predicate concepts in judgments like 'A straight line is the shortest distance between two points,' 'The sum of the angles of a triangle = 180', seem not to be amenable to analysis in such a way that the judgments are recursively analytic. That for Kant a judgment with a complex subject concept is analytic only if the predicate of the judgment can be derived from an analysis of the subject concept into its components; i.e., only if it is *recursively* analytic, is indicated by the following remark. "Take, for instance, the proposition, 'Two straight lines cannot enclose a space, and with them alone no figure is possible' *and try to derive it from the concept of straight lines and of the number two* [italics mine] (CPR, A 48, B 65, p. 86; see also A 164, B 205, p. 199). We have already indicated that the metaphysical judgments expressing the conclusions of the Analogies are also emergently analytic.

The principal use to which Kant puts the distinction between analytic and synthetic judgments is in relation to the nature of metaphysics. Analytic judgments are merely *explicative,* whereas synthetic judgments are *ampliative* (i.e., extend our knowledge). Metaphysics is, in intent, both a priori and ampliative (CPR, pp. 55–56) and so requires a priori ampliative judgments. What Kant was reacting against was the kind of metaphysical or philosophical analysis carried on by the Leibnizian school. According to Leibniz, in order to see what follows from a complex concept, break up the concept into simpler parts and see what predicates follow separately from these parts. This conception would always result in what we have called recursively analytic judgments that, for Kant, are merely explicative. Kant's procedure, on the other hand, is quite different. He would not analyze more complex concepts into simpler ones, but rather compound more simple concepts into more complex ones and derive predicates not derivable from the simpler concepts separately. This procedure results in what we have called *emergent* analytic judgments, which are ampliative. The "trick" in this procedure was to see what concepts could serve as "third somethings = x" so that, when combined with the subject concept, they would yield predicates not derivable from the subject concept alone or from the concept serving as the "third something" alone. To see that not any concepts could serve in this way as third somethings, consider the following example. Start with the concept 'bachelor' and let the concept 'bald' be the third something. Then any predicate 'P' derivable from the concept 'bald bachelor' is such that it is derivable from one of these concepts alone ('unmarried man') or it is analyzable into components that are so derivable ('unmarried-man-without-hair'). In this sense, we get no *emergent* predicates by using 'bald' as the third something. Based on this example, it might seem that the method of compounding concepts rather than breaking them up into components is also merely explicative. And yet Kant thought that in metaphysics he had found a concept that could serve as a third something in a fruitful manner (in such a way that it could generate what we have called emergent analytic judgments), viz., the concept of the possibility of experience, or the concept of determinability. For example, the predicate 'is caused' is not derivable from the concept of a temporal event, but it is derivable from the concept of a temporal-event-determinable-as-such, or the concept of an event-determinable-as-having-a-position-in-time.

The burden of giving a characterization of *simple* versus *complex* concepts in terms of which the distinction between recursive and emergent analytic judgments was formulated can perhaps be bypassed if we understand that Kant was addressing himself to the Leibnizian conception of analysis that took this distinction as understood.* It is on these, Leibniz's own, terms that Kant sees the possibility of an alternative to the Leibnizian method of analysis (dissolution), by the making more complex (the synthesis) of a subject concept in order to enable the derivation of *emergent* predicate concepts. Finally, the distinction between recursive and emergent analyticity is not a psychological distinction between what is *obviously* thought in the subject concept from what is *unobviously* thought. Careful consideration and analysis may be required to see that a judgment is recursively analytic, yet this analysis is still only explicative, never ampliative, in that it can never give rise to what we have called emergent predicates.

If we return to Lewis's standard of adequacy, we see that although it makes all judgments whose concepts are necessarily connected

---

* In any case, the formulation really requires no more than the *relative* notions of *more* and *less* simple, which do not seem implausible.

ipso facto into analytic judgments, it does not make them all into recursive analytic judgments. We may, if we wish, agree to label judgments like 'A four-sided equiangular figure has its diagonals equal' or 'An event determinable as temporal is caused' analytic since the predicate concept is necessarily connected with the subject concept and hence on Lewis's standard of adequacy is to be considered as forming part of the complete subject concept. Nevertheless, they are not emergent analytic judgments in that their truth is not arrived at using the Leibnizian method of analysis, but rather by using the method of complexification (synthesis) of simpler concepts; i.e., by the addition of a concept serving as a third something in terms of which emergent predicates follow. Hence they are ampliative rather than explicative judgments. In other words, they have all the characteristics that, for Kant, would make them synthetic judgments.

Selected Bibliography

WORKS BY KANT

Critique of Pure Reason, edited and translated by Norman Kemp Smith. London: Macmillan & Co., 1963.

Kritik der reinen Vernuft, edited by Benno Erdmann. Berlin: Georg Reiner, 1900.

Gesammette Schriften. Berlin and Leipzig: Preussischen Akademie der Wissenchaften, 1938.

Band IV, *Prolegomena*

Band V, *Kritik der Urteilskraft*

Band XXI, XXII, *Kants Handschriftlicher Nachlass*

Critique of Judgment, translated by J. H. Bernard. New York & London: Hafner Publishing Co., 1966.

Philosophical Correspondence 1759–1799, edited by Arnulf Zweig. Chicago: University of Chicago Press, 1967.

Prolegomena to Any Future Metaphysics, edited by Paul Carus. Chicago: Open Court, 1902.

Selected Pre-Critical Writings and Correspondence with Beck, edited by G. B. Kerferd and D. E. Walford. New York: Barnes and Noble, 1968.

Reflexionen Kants, edited by Benno Erdmann. Leipzig: R. Riesland, 1884.

OTHER WORKS CITED

Bennett, Jonathan. *Kant's Analytic.* Cambridge: Cambridge University Press, 1966.

Bird, Graham. *Kant's Theory of Knowledge.* London: Routledge & Kegan Paul, 1962.

Cassirer, H. W. *A Commentary on Kant's Critique of Judgment.* London: Methuen & Co. Ltd., 1938.

Hume, David. *A Treatise of Human Nature,* edited by Selby-Bigge. Oxford: Oxford University Press, 1888.

Kemp Smith, Norman. *A Commentary to Kant's 'Critique of Pure Reason.'* London: Macmillan & Co., 1918.

Lewis, C. I. *An Analysis of Knowledge & Valuation.* LaSalle, Ill.: Open Court, 1946.

Lovejoy, Arthur. "On Kant's Reply to Hume," *Archiv für Geschichte der Philosophie,* 1906. Reprinted in *Kant: Disputed Questions,* edited by Moltke S. Gram. Chicago: Quadrangle Books, 1967.

Paton, H. J. *Kant's Metaphysic of Experience.* 2 vols. New York: Macmillan & Co., 1936.

Quine, Willard Van Orman, *Word and Object.* Cambridge, Mass.: M.I.T. Press, 1960.

Strawson, Peter. *The Bounds of Sense.* London: Methuen & Co., Ltd., 1966.

Stroud, Barry. "Transcendental Arguments." *Journal of Philosophy* 65 (May 1968). Reprinted in *The First Critique,* edited by T. Penelhum and J. J. MacIntosh. Belmont, Calif.: Wadsworth Publishing Co., Inc., 1969.

————. "Review of *Ludwig Wittgenstein:* David Pears." *Journal of Philosophy* 79 (January 1972).

Swing, Thomas Kaeho. *Kant's Transcendental Logic.* New Haven: Yale University Press, 1969.

Vaihinger, Hans. *Kommentar zu Kants Kritik der Reinen Vernunft,* Stuttgart: W. Spennan, 1881 and 1892.

Warnock, G. J. "Every Event Has a Cause." *Logic and Language,* edited by Anthony Flew. Oxford: Basil Blackwell, 1961.

Wolff, Robert Paul. *Kant's Theory of Mental Activity.* Cambridge, Mass.: Harvard University Press, 1963.

OTHER BOOKS CONSULTED

Caird, Edward. *The Critical Philosophy of Immanuel Kant.* Vol. 1. Glasgow: J. Maclehose & Sons, 1909.

Dryer, Douglas. *Kant's Solution for Verification in Metaphysics.* London: Allen & Unwin, 1966.

Ewing, A. C. *A Short Commentary on Kant's Critique of Pure Reason.* Chicago: University of Chicago Press, 1938.
———. *Kant's Treatment of Causality.* London: K. Paul, Trench, Trubner & Co., 1924.
Prichard, H. A. *Kant's Theory of Knowledge.* Oxford: Clarendon Press, 1909.
Sellars, Wilfrid. *Science and Metaphysics.* New York: Humanities Press, 1968.
Sidgwick, Henry. *Lectures on the Philosophy of Kant.* London: Macmillan & Co., 1905.
Weldon, T. D. *An Examination of Kant's Critique of Pure Reason.* Oxford: Clarendon Press, 1958.

OTHER ARTICLES CONSULTED

Beck, Lewis White. "Can Kant's Synthetic Judgments Be Made Analytic?" *Kant-Studien* 47 (1956). Reprinted in *Kant: A Collection of Critical Essays,* edited by R. P. Wolff. New York: Doubleday & Co., Inc., 1967.
———. "Kant's Theory of Definition." *Philosophical Review* 65 (1956). Reprinted in *Kant: A Collection of Critical Essays,* edited by R. P. Wolff.
———. "The Second Analogy and the Principle of Indeterminacy." *Kant-Studien* 57 (1966). Reprinted in *The First Critique,* edited by T. Penelhum & J. J. MacIntosh.
———. "Once More Unto the Breach." *Ratio* 9 (June 1967).
———. "Rejoinder to Professors Murphy and Williams." *Ratio* 11 (June 1969).
Kopper, J. "Kants Zweite Analogie der Erfahrung." *Kant-Studien* 61 (1970).
Murphy, Jeffrie G. "Kant's Second Analogy as an Answer to Hume." *Ratio* 11 (June 1969).
Neisser, Hans P. "Are Space and Time Real?" *Philosophy and Phenomenological Research* 31 (March 1971).
Parsons, Charles D. "Infinity and Kant's Conception of the 'Possibility Of Experience.'" *Philosophical Review* 73 (1964). Reprinted in *Kant: A Collection of Critical Essays,* edited by R. P. Wolff.

Robinson, Richard. "Necessary Propositions." *Mind* (1958). Reprinted in *The First Critique*. Edited by T. Penelhum & J. J. MacIntosh.

Schipper, E. W. "Kant's Answer to Hume's Problem." *Kant-Studien* 53 (1961–62).

Schrader, George. "The Transcendental Ideality and Empirical Reality of Kant's Space and Time." *Review of Metaphysics* (1950–51).

――――. "The Status of Teleological Judgment in the Critical Philosophy." *Kant-Studien* (1953–54).

Stegmüller, W. "Towards A Rational Reconstruction of Kant's Metaphysics of Experience. Part II: The Logical Structure of the Progressive Argument." *Ratio* 10 (June 1968).

Suchting, W. A. "Kant's Second Analogy of Experience." *Kant-Studien* 58 (1967). Reprinted in *Kant Studies Today*, edited by L. W. Beck. LaSalle, Ill.: Open Court, 1969.

Tonelli, G. "Die Anfänge von Kants Kritik der Kausalbeziehung und ihre Voraussetzungen im 18. Jahrhundert." *Kant-Studien* 57 (1966).

Walsh, W. H. "Categories." *Kant-Studien* 45 (1954). Reprinted in *Kant: A Collection of Critical Essays,* edited by R. P. Wolff.

――――. "Schematism." *Kant-Studien* 49 (1957). Reprinted in *Kant: A Collection of Critical Essays.*

――――. "Kant on the Perception of Time." *Monist* (1967). Reprinted in *The First Critique,* edited by T. Penelhum & J. J. MacIntosh, and in *Kant Studies Today,* edited by L. W. Beck.

Williams, M. E. "Kant's Reply to Hume." *Kant-Studien* 56 (1965).

――――. "The Breach Again." *Ratio* 11 (June 1969).

Index